17.95

Kathleen Y. Ritter, PhD
Craig W. O'Neill, STD

Righteous Religion: Unmasking the Illusions of Fundamentalism and Authoritarian Catholicism

Pre-publication
REVIEWS,
COMMENTARIES,
EVALUATIONS . . .

"**R**ighteous Religion offers both trenchant analysis and reassuring counsel on how to deal with faith traditions that 'father' their adherents. The authors name duplicity and clergy immaturity in patriarchal churches as contributing factors to the Protestantism and undifferentiated Roman Catholicism.

This lethal combination kills the spirit in many people and causes an exodus from such churches. The development of adult faith requires thinking for oneself and seeing religious institutions as fallible. Then, readers will find healthy, thinking people can be religious with rewarding results."

Mary E. Hunt, PhD
Co-Director,
Women's Alliance for Theology,
Ethics, and Ritual (WATER),
Silver Spring, Maryland

"**R**itter and O'Neill have written an extraordinary book dedicated to the insight that whatever is bad psychology must be bad theology and vice versa. The issue is not true religion versus false religion, but pathological versus healthy religion. If, as St. Iraneus said in the fourth century, 'The Glory of God are humans fully alive,' then any religion that is destructive to human psychological and spiritual development is, by that fact, false religion that denies God His/Her glory.

Ritter and O'Neill identify the destructive patterns that characterize authoritarian religion, whether of the Fundamentalist or Catholic variety, patterns that repeat the failings of dysfunctional families.

They also outline the growth process by which individuals escape the destructiveness of pathological religion by overcoming illusions, withdrawing from their embeddedness in the community by a mourning process. They proceed to integrate their spiritual values into an autonomous and mature self.

The use of case histories brings all the issues alive in a dramatic and clear way. The message of this book is that we cannot become one with the divine through a false self trying to please external authority. We can only become one with the divine by becoming one with the mature, healthy, and authentic self."

John J. McNeill, PhD
Psychotherapist,
New York, New York

The Haworth Pastoral Press
An Imprint of The Haworth Press, Inc.

Righteous Religion
Unmasking the Illusions
of Fundamentalism
and Authoritarian Catholicism

The Haworth Pastoral Press
Religion , Ministry & Pastoral Care
William M. Clements, PhD
Senior Editor

New, Recent, and Forthcoming Titles:

Growing Up: Pastoral Nurture for the Later Years by Thomas B. Robb

Religion and the Family: When God Helps by Laurel Arthur Burton

Victims of Dementia: Services, Support, and Care by Wm. Michael Clemmer

Horrific Traumata: A Pastoral Response to the Post-Traumatic Stress Disorder by N. Duncan Sinclair

Aging and God: Spiritual Pathways to Mental Health in Midlife and Later Years by Harold G. Koenig

Counseling for Spiritually Empowered Wholeness: A Hope-Centered Approach by Howard Clinebell

Shame: A Faith Perspective by Robert H. Albers

Dealing with Depression: Five Pastoral Interventions by Richard Dayringer

Righteous Religion: Unmasking the Illusions of Fundamentalism and Authoritarian Catholicism by Kathleen Y. Ritter and Craig W. O'Neill

Righteous Religion
Unmasking the Illusions of Fundamentalism and Authoritarian Catholicism

Kathleen Y. Ritter, PhD
Craig W. O'Neill, STD

The Haworth Pastoral Press
An Imprint of The Haworth Press, Inc.
New York • London

Published by

The Haworth Pastoral Press, an imprint of The Haworth Press, Inc., 10 Alice Street, Binghamton, NY 13904-1580

Library of Congress Cataloging-in-Publication Data

Ritter, Kathleen.
   Righteous religion : unmasking the illusions of Fundamentalism and Authoritarian Catholicism / Kathleen Y. Ritter, Craig W. O'Neill.
      p.   cm.
   Includes bibliographical references and index.
   ISBN 0-7890-6016-7 (alk. paper)
   1. Fanaticism–Controversial literature. 2. Fundamentalism–Controversial literature. 3. Catholic Church–Controversial literature. 4. Faith development. 5. Christianity–Psychology. I. O'Neill, Craig. II. Title.
BR114.R57   1996
270.8'29–dc20   96-4734
                                                                          CIP

To our partners, John and Mikel

ABOUT THE AUTHORS

Kathleen Yost Ritter, PhD, is Professor of Counseling at California State University and a psychotherapist in private practice at the Westchester Counseling Center in Bakersfield, California. Dr. Ritter has served on the editorial boards of several national journals, and is the author of numerous articles that have appeared in professional journals, including *Human Development* and the *Journal of Counseling and Development*. For the past five years, she has served as a presenter for the American Counseling Association's national workshop series and has conducted workshops in numerous U.S. cities. Together with Craig William O'Neill, PhD, she has presented papers on spiritual topics to the Western Psychological Association, the American Academy of Religion, and the American Psychological Association.

Craig William O'Neill, STD, PhD, is Spiritual Director at the Center for Sacred Psychology in Los Angeles, California, and also extends his practice to Bakersfield, California. A former Roman Catholic Priest, Dr. O'Neill worked in parishes in the San Joaquin Valley of California for 16 years. He has taught courses on meditation and collaborative ministry at Loyola Marymount University and has lectured extensively on topics related to spirituality and Catholicism. He and Kathleen Yost Ritter, PhD, co-authored *Coming Out Within* and have written several articles on spirituality for the *Journal of Counseling and Development*. Dr. O'Neill's interests include spirituality, mysticism, rituals, and meditation.

CONTENTS

PART THREE: CLAIMING YOUR OWN VOICE

Preface

As a psychotherapist and a priest/spiritual director, we have listened to innumerable people describe their disillusionment and struggles with authoritarian religion. Their shared experiences caused us to reflect on why so many individuals are discouraged and even spiritually blocked, many times in spite of being active participants in their churches. Their dilemmas and our own have compelled us to write *Righteous Religion*.

Having met Catholics and Protestants who have told us essentially the same stories, we came to realize that many similar elements existed in both religious traditions. Likewise, we soon understood that it wasn't the *fundamentals* of these Christian belief systems that constituted the problem, but rather, the authoritarian *misuse* of these fundamentals. In other words, the heart of Christian teaching is sound and valuable; the difficulty is in how it is transmitted. Therefore, having much the same message for the two populations, we decided to write the book for both groups.

Righteous Religion assists readers in understanding the grip that authoritarian practices within Fundamentalism and Catholicism have on people in spite of financial and sexual scandals, misuse of power and influence, apparent hypocrisy and selective self-righteousness. It examines the dynamics of these belief systems and the control they exercise on the imagination and loyalty of believers. Further, it unmasks the parental and familial illusions that shape the face and character of authoritarian religion. The immense holding power of these churches is best understood by comparing it with the intimate bond between children and their parents. In the minds of believers, Catholicism and Fundamentalism assume the role of nurturing parents who speak with the voice of God on earth. Quite naturally, members expect these parents to foster healthy families which abide by Judeo-Christian principles. In their faith-families, they expect to be treated justly, listened to, communicated with, and to enjoy the authority of leaders who are capable of these qualities. Righteous religion, then, reinforces such illusions by presenting itself in parental language and using familial terms.

In spite of the unmistakable popularity and growth of authoritarian churches, it is the premise of *Righteous Religion* that all is not well beneath the surface of Fundamentalism and Catholicism. Millions of people are disillusioned with their experiences in these faiths and with parenting that is far from ideal. Members of authoritarian churches often reside in a religious atmosphere where the threat of exclusion from the heavenly home is a pervasive reality and where fear, guilt, and shame are commonly used tools to keep wayward believers under control and faithfully dependent. Living in an environment with such negative parenting eventually wears thin and many people come to feel invalidated, cheated, frustrated, betrayed, and even saddened.

The sense of disillusionment frequently is intensified when Catholics and Fundamentalists become aware of the nature of the system in which this self-righteous parenting takes place. When the dissonance between what the church purports to be and what many members actually experience and observe becomes apparent, the feelings of disillusionment are further exacerbated.

What many people are beginning to perceive is that parenting, while it may have served them well at one time, now lacks the flexibility to adapt to their personal and spiritual development. Further, they often see a system that seems to fragment the family, stifles the voices of its members, and undermines the very stability it so desires. Particularly troubling to them may be the parental church's efforts to bind its children tightly to itself, make excessive and rigid demands for loyalty, and scapegoat members who differ from the norm or who try to surface the family secrets.

The communication process within authoritarian churches often leaves members feeling talked down to, ignored, and bereft of their own voices of truth. Through the use of true-to-life stories of ordinary people, *Righteous Religion* demonstrates that the efforts involved in maintaining illusions are incompatible with claiming a spiritual voice. This book discusses the relationship between the deconstruction of illusions and the growth involved in finding a voice of one's own. The journey from holding unquestioned assumptions about religion to the transformation of these illusions covers a large emotional territory, which is described for readers.

Some definition of terms seems to be in order at this point. When we refer to authoritarian practices or authoritarian churches, we are referring to religion that presents itself as overly self-assured, dogmatic, imperative, controlling, domineering, and dictatorial. Obviously, not all expressions of Catholicism and Protestantism are framed in this manner. The focus of our book is directed toward the aspects of these religious traditions that are manifestly self-righteous. Thus, the title *Righteous Religion*.

When describing an authoritarian subset of Protestantism, we elected to use the term Fundamentalism, which is commonly understood as a movement that began in the early twentieth century as a reaction to cultural change and liberal biblical interpretation. The term "fundamentalist" is often used in the United States to describe individuals who espouse the authority of sacred scripture. While this term is more commonly descriptive of a theological affirmation than a group identification, *Righteous Religion* employs the Fundamentalist designation to refer to individuals whose faith is rooted deeply in God as God speaks through the Bible, and whose religious practices are exercised through churches which provide them with community as well as clarification in applying scripture. Belief, morality, and worship are centered on the printed word, which must be read literally, and a "born again" in Christ experience is considered essential by the majority. Fundamentalists, thus, believe that the original Hebrew and Greek manuscripts of the Bible are without error and that they tell Christians all that God wills to tell them and all they need to know for salvation and eternal life.

While the above description may apply to Evangelical as well as Fundamentalist traditions, many within mainstream Evangelical churches choose to disassociate themselves from the latter. For example, many Fundamentalists would not seek membership in the National Association of Evangelicals, support humanitarian organizations, or read *Christianity Today* magazine. Fundamentalist churches are often independent, autonomous groups which, unlike conventional Evangelical churches or mainstream Protestantism, tend to emphasize personal salvation over social concerns and world peace, warfare rather than religious harmony, and the superiority of their beliefs over and above those of others, even within Protestantism. Perhaps, the most important distinction, however, is what many perceive as an exceedingly authoritarian approach to this exercise of religion.

The lines which divide smaller units of conservative Protestants are often blurred. Our use of the term Fundamentalist is not perfect but seems to be the best choice available, given its widespread use for describing a certain flavor of Protestantism. We also acknowledge that there are certain factions within Catholicism who could be described as fundamentalists, given the authoritarian nature of their religious practices. For the purposes of this book, however, we have restricted the term Fundamentalist to Protestants.

Catholics, much like Protestants, do not constitute a homogeneous group. But unlike conservative Protestantism, there are no subset group designations (such as Evangelical or Fundamentalist) available and in common usage. Thus, in *Righteous Religion*, when we refer to Catholicism, we mean those expressions of Catholicism that are dogmatic, self-righteous, dictatorial, and authoritarian. We are well aware that another, more vibrant form of Catholicism coexists, as evidenced by the Documents of Vatican II and much current practice within the Catholic Church. Recent documents (1995, 1984) from the official church, however, continue to stress its authoritarian nature.

Righteous Religion describes many experiences in the lives of Fundamentalists and Catholics. Some of these are painful and do not always present churches or organized religion in the most favorable light. In telling these stories, we attempted to be accurate in our description of events, yet respectful of the individuals involved. In this regard, we ask readers to keep in mind that churches not only shape personalities, but that people gravitate toward those religious traditions that meet their needs. In the case of those people who find authoritarian religion attractive, undoubtedly their requirements for certainty, authority, safety, and absolute and definitive answers are acknowledged. For many, their church may be the only place in their lives where they find these kinds of reassurances.

We wish to express our gratitude to those individuals who have told their stories of disillusionment and who have compelled us to make sense of their struggles of faith. We extend our appreciation also to those sacred people who have guided our spiritual paths as we have waded through the morass of righteous religion. We both thank Father Patrick Hannon and Craig acknowledges the inspiration of Betsy Caprio and the staff at the Center for Sacred Psychology in Los Angeles.

Our endeavor has been helped by the dedicated assistance of those at The Haworth Press, particularly Dr. William M. Clements, Senior Editor; William Palmer, Managing Editor; Christine Matthews, Administrative Assistant; Susan Trzeciak, Administrative Editor; Dawn Krisko, Production Editor; Peg Marr, Senior Production Editor; Lisa Franko, Copy Editor; Patricia Brown, Production Manager; and Marylouise Doyle, Cover Designer. Thanks also to the Reprographics staff at California State University, Bakersfield, especially Aggie Arvizu, Carolyn Alexander, and Julie White for their production assistance. Steve Devore, Lyn and Robert Scales, and Richard Erickson helped refine our thinking regarding Evangelical/Fundamentalist Protestantism.

Introduction

At the 10:00 a.m. service at a midtown church, there sat eight individuals in the ninth row, lefthand side. During the course of the worship, all of them were struggling with thoughts about their church and conflicts they were having with it and its leaders.

Dana sat next to the center aisle. The preceding Tuesday she had had an abortion. The pains caused by the procedure still reverberated through her body but were minimal compared with the emotional pain she was feeling. Over the years, in this very church, she had heard preachers repeatedly describe people such as herself as murderers. Dana was certain that none of the staff here at the church would understand, much less sympathize, with her side of the story. Could they really understand how attracted she was to Jason and how resolutely she had tried not having sex with him over the past six months? Could they fathom the terror she felt when she learned she was pregnant and how fearful she was of hurting her mother? Additionally, the news would have killed her dad. She had taken Jason's money for the abortion so that her family would not find out. Having made a conscious choice to terminate the pregnancy, she refused to feel contaminated as she sat among these good Christians. Her isolation, however, was intense since the church apparently didn't want people like her nor would the pastor support her once he found out about the sin she had committed. She desperately wanted to worship with a community of fellow believers and decided not to let the judgment of others prevent her from doing so.

Jack and **Olivia**, sitting next to Dana, were dealing with their own form of exclusion that morning. Only yesterday, they had visited the pastor and were told that due to Olivia's previous marriage and divorce, he in conscience could not marry them. Jack had been a member of this congregation all of his life and had helped raise money for the church when it was being constructed. Having dated quite a few women, he realized that Olivia was his true life mate. Yet to the mind of the pastor, she belonged to another man and thus their relationship was adulterous. The injustice of the situation assaulted him as he sat at the 10:00 a.m. service. He felt spurned in his own home and forced to marry outside of the church if he wanted to stay with Olivia. Throughout the ceremony, he prayed about his situation. By the end of the service, he was still firm in his resolution to marry Olivia—wherever that might be. He further resolved to remain with the congregation, to consider himself fully included in the church family, and to begin defining membership on his own terms.

James sat further down the pew. He, like Jack, felt equally excluded. James was gay and in a relationship with Jeff. Numerous times he had tried to talk himself out of attending services, but somehow the mystery, the memories, and the traditions had drawn him back. Sundays were often extremely unpleasant for him, however. For example, only a month ago, the pastor gave a sermon characterizing heterosexuality as harmonious with God's plan for "mankind" and homosexuality as a perverted and sinful choice. James could barely contain his outrage. It seemed as if he were continually struggling to maintain his sense of acceptability in the face of the church's condemnation of gay and lesbian sexuality and relationships. Wanting to feel included in the Christian family and inspired spiritually, he put aside old feelings of fear, guilt, and unworthiness, and decided to partake in communion with the other members of the congregation.

Laura, sitting next to James, felt as excluded and alienated as James as she counted the twenty-seventh male reference in the service. Not a soul leading the service was female. She was not impressed when the pastor congratulated the women of the congregation for decorating the previous Saturday's appreciation luncheon honoring members of various church committees. Laura was sick and tired of hearing this man overidealize women, while at the same time failing to provide them any means to influence the organization's decision making or participate in the services.

She had played an instrumental role on the regional committee which had been convened to serve as a forum for the role of women in the church. Laura organized meetings in several congregations in order to allow women as much input as possible regarding their concerns about the church. After many months of work and numerous hours crafting the language, the committee's report was ready to be presented to a board of pastors in open forum. On the day of the meeting, the committee chairman's earlier openness seemed to have disappeared when he stood before them and made his opening remarks. He informed them that he was eager to hear the comments but that certain issues were unacceptable for discussion, namely the criticizing of the so-called "patriarchal" structure of their church organization, changes in the language of worship, and expanded roles for women in the church. His guidelines virtually eviscerated the paper Laura's group had worked so hard to assemble. Sitting in the pew that Sunday, she still remembered the anger and frustration that caused her to rise to her feet at the meeting and give voice to her feelings of being discounted and devalued. Her sense of justice was deeply offended when the chairman responded to her with the words, "My dear, please be seated. We must all behave like brothers and sisters in Christ."

Benjamin, a prominent member of the finance committee, occupied the pew next to Laura. Similar to her, he lately had been frustrated by the one-way channels of communication in the church. The pastor treated the committee as a rubber stamp for his plans and had informed his inner circle that he wouldn't bother with such a group if it hadn't been mandated by his superior. By controlling the agenda and dominating the meetings, the pastor left the committee members with the sense that they had been manipulated and disrespected. Benjamin, a successful businessman, had been elected for his financial expertise. Yet not once had he been consulted on the budget, which the pastor considered to be his private domain. Benjamin seethed with anger as he recalled the frequency with which the pastor invited the committee's input into the congregation's functioning and how rarely he listened to it.

As Benjamin tried to pray that Sunday, his thoughts about his membership on the committee kept intruding. Looking up again at the pastor droning on, it became clear to Benjamin that he needed to let him know the extent of his discontent. He decided to call the church office the next day for an appointment.

Betty, sitting next to Benjamin, was having thoughts about clergy. She had been a member of the church all of her seventy-three years. The pastors she remembered from her younger years seemed to have been better and more stable. They and the church seemed to have so many problems these days. Her children and grandchildren had stopped going to services altogether and told her that they felt the church had made itself irrelevant with its seemingly excessive focus on power, prohibitions, and sexual matters. They said they experienced more spiritual inspiration from family brunches or communing with nature.

It saddened her that they had given up on the church so young in life and that the Christian heritage, which had passed through so many generations of her family, may be ending with her. When she tried reasoning with her children and grandchildren and encouraging them to remain in the church to make it more relevant, they told her that this was pointless because the church wasn't listening to its members anyway. The argument struck home with Betty because she had been noticing much the same thing lately. Consequently, when the time for the offering came, she chose to keep the money in her purse and donate a comparable amount to the senior citizens' center.

Bennet, the brother of a pastor, occupied the end of the pew. He was feeling particularly disgruntled with the church this morning because his brother, Gary, had just been terminated at another congregation for the second time in two years. Bennet had always acted protectively toward his younger brother who had been the only one left at home with Mother when Dad died. It had been one of Dad's strongest hopes that Gary would enter the ministry and Gary had honored his father's wish. In the ten years since ordination, Gary had struggled with depression and Bennet knew it was because his brother was lonely and in a career that was ill-suited to his personality. Often Gary would go home to drink after the evening's activities at the church were completed. He acquired the reputation with church officials for being a liability among the clergy and moved frequently from one distant outpost to another. It angered and hurt Bennet how the church had used Gary's ministry over the years yet had offered him neither a promotion to pastor nor help with his problems. Only when Gary's drinking or depression became severe did his superiors approve the three weeks' mental health treatment allowed by the insurance carrier. On those few occasions when Gary had asked for a more extended leave, the request was denied due to a lack of available funding for clergy rehabilitation. These were Bennet's thoughts as he sat at the 10:00 a.m. service and listened to the pastor reflecting on the joy of his life in ministry. The more Bennet heard about the blessings granted by the church to this pastor, the more conflicted and tormented he became. To him, the church seemed hypocritical in that it treated some clergy very honorably with the right hand, and discarded others with the left. He became so uncomfortable listening to this mixed message that he finally got up and left.

The eight people in pew nine are experiencing a variety of painful emotions as they grapple with their relationship with their church. Obviously, their faith is important to them, otherwise they wouldn't be there on Sunday morning. We believe that in many ways, they are representative of a large number of Christians who are also feeling conflicted about their religion. Similar to Dana, Jack, Olivia, James, Laura, Benjamin, Betty, and Bennet, an increasing number of religiously bonded people are experiencing many of the feelings described below:

- unsafe in a congregation or denomination that is no longer responsive to their emotional and spiritual needs;
- invalidated when their goodness is not reflected back to them by the religious organization;
- abandoned by a church that once promised to stand by them through "thick and thin";
- apprehensive about their acceptability and fearful of potential exclusion;
- distressed and guilty at not being able to achieve unattainable standards of behavior;
- shameful, unworthy, and defective despite their best efforts;
- evil and sinful when their genuine and honest emotions are discredited;
- devalued when their efforts at maturing and finding their own voices are undermined;
- frustrated and inhibited when their voices are suppressed by their religion;
- thwarted when there are no channels for negotiation of differences;

- stifled when attempting to openly address congregational or denominational conflicts and issues;
- disinherited for being different;
- cast out when they must leave the organization for the sake of their own integrity;
- discounted and minimized by the efforts of the religious body to maintain its authority and equilibrium;
- left out and ignored;
- caught in a system of contradictory and mixed messages;
- disempowered by religion's exercise of top-down, unilateral power;
- offended when their sense of justice is continually challenged by the actions of the parental church;
- exiled from/in their own home; and
- saddened that a religious organization willfully alienates its own children in order to preserve itself.

RELIGIOUS ILLUSIONS

An element common to the eight people in the pew is that all of them are grappling with some degree of disillusionment. Their illusions regarding the church's ability to meet their needs on the deepest level are beginning to erode. People who have bonded with their religious organization and who have come to trust it possess a belief that in many ways it stands in the place of, and thus speaks for, God. As they move through life, many come to realize that the voice of the church and the voice of God are quite different, and that numerous expectations of the church and the workings of the organization are contrary to what their intuition tells them about God's spirit. This clash between their illusions and the actual practices of the religious organization leads to disillusionment.

Whether consciously or unconsciously, most members expect justice from their religion (i.e., I do my part, you will do yours). They trust that if they do the best they can, the church will reciprocate as a nurturing parent who fosters a functioning family. Along these lines, many believers hold to the illusions that the church, like a good parent, will:

- provide for lifelong and eternal inclusion;
- calm fears (rather than intensify them);
- quell guilt;
- enhance their sense of acceptability;
- reduce unworthiness and shame;
- encourage and support them in finding their own voices; and
- respect their maturity and assist them in their spiritual growth.

Religiously bonded individuals expect to live in a family that is healthy and abides by Judeo-Christian principles, but they are frequently disillusioned by the way the church operates as a family. They may hold to the additional illusions that the parental church:

- is "above" the problems of human families;
- does not resort to underhanded methods in order to reduce stress and tension in the family system;
- has no secrets;
- conducts its business openly and above board;
- treats its members justly;
- selects leaders who are approachable and open to dialogue;
- appoints leaders who are mature, healthy, and emotionally balanced;
- listens to the voice of its children;
- encourages two-way communication;
- strives to send clear, congruent, and noncontradictory messages; and
- promotes congregations characterized by equanimity and goodwill.

For each person seated in pew nine, lefthand side, an unpleasant demise of illusions is occurring that Sunday morning. For example, every one of them is feeling a sense of exclusion for themselves or someone close to them. In addition, Dana, Jack, Olivia, and James are struggling to overcome their emotions of fear, guilt, unworthiness, and shame. Each of the eight, of course, wants to feel some degree of support, understanding, acceptability, and peace in the spiritual home as they deal with very painful circumstances. They all once had the illusion that their religion would encourage and support them as they contended with difficult decisions of life and conscience.

Likewise, the individuals in our hypothetical pew are dealing with broken hopes regarding the church as a functional family. At some level, they all want to be treated justly, listened to, communicated with, and to respect the authority of leaders who are capable of these qualities. Laura, Benjamin, and Bennet, in particular, have had personal encounters with a system that shattered their illusions that the church can deal with them in a clear, aboveboard, and mature manner.

AUTHORITARIAN RELIGION

What these eight people could probably agree upon is that they are having severe misgivings about their church and are grappling with its teaching and functioning. Just as many other disillusioned believers, they are encountering a denomination or local congregation whose primary focus appears to be on eliminating dissension, maintaining control within that organization, and raising money. *Righteous Religion* refers to those congregations which, like whitened tombs, appear upright, virtuous, and whitewashed on the outside and yet on the inside are filled with hypocrisy and dead [men's] bones (Matthew 23:27-28).[1] From the perspective of the late twentieth century, these "bones" might refer to a dogmatic approach to theology, self-righteousness, authoritarian use of power, a refusal to entertain conflicting views, arrogance, and sometimes even duplicity. Such religious organizations are often blindly self-assured and presumptuous as they ask their members to sacrifice personal growth for the sake of religious cohesion and uniformity. If there is a difference of opinion, the church self-confidently presumes that the problem or the error is with the believer and not with the institution. Members of such churches often sense the subtle (and sometimes not-so-subtle) force of moral imperatives and the conspiracies of silence around definitions of loyalty or who may participate and how.

Some readers may find themselves feeling suffocated in these whitened tombs, almost as if their spirit is being extinguished by the irrelevant rules, tightened controls, and ecclesial hypocrisy they see around them. Others are experiencing a myriad of conflicting emotions regarding their faith community. Some are demoralized by the church's moral dictates, and many are simply amused by or indifferent to the travesty of religion's blind guides leading the blindly trusting (Matthew 23:24).[2]

GROWING PAINS

Righteous Religion is built upon the premise that the dilemmas and discouragement being faced by so many believers are part of the process of their spiritual growth. These very same dilemmas constitute the catalyst for members to move beyond their illusions about authoritarian religion and to claim their own spiritual voices, that is, to speak from their own experience of God who resides within them.

With maturity (or when events such as an abortion, divorce, or coming out occur), some people begin to comprehend the extent to which illusions are intertwined and incorporated throughout their belief systems. As children, they learned to trust innocently in all that the church taught and absorbed both truth and illusion, without questioning either. With adulthood and its accompanying traumas and challenges, they are more often confronted with the discrepancies between their illusions and the sometimes unsavory reality of the religious organization.

The eight people sitting side by side on Sunday morning, while not able to prevent their illusions from crumbling, are utilizing the pain of a particular difficulty to take responsibility for their own lives and decisions. In other words, they acted upon an opportunity to assume their own voice. For example, Dana refused to shoulder the church's shaming when she made a decision of conscience about terminating her pregnancy. Olivia and Jack chose to honor their love for each other and thus to define inclusion in their own way. By receiving communion that morning, James affirmed his acceptability in the eyes of God as a gay man, as well as his inherent place in the faith community. Laura felt she was making a statement about her own empowerment as a Christian simply by being there that Sunday morning considering how the chairman had tried to stifle her voice a few days earlier. Similar to her, Benjamin felt equally disempowered but intended to voice his concerns to the pastor in the future. Betty expressed herself in a less vocal yet highly effective way when she shut her purse at collection time. Bennet demonstrated his displeasure at the church's duplicity in regards to the treatment of its clergy, particularly his brother, by walking out of the sermon.

CLAIMING YOUR OWN VOICE

A primary thesis of this book is that the efforts involved in maintaining illusions are incompatible with claiming a voice of spiritual truth. It is impossible to view the world through the distorting lens of illusions while at the same looking inward to the soul and deeper self. *Righteous Religion* discusses the relationship between the deconstruction of illusions and the growth involved in finding the voice of the spirit within. The journey from holding unquestioned assumptions about religion to the transformation of these illusions covers a large emotional territory, which will be described for readers.

The book is organized around an introductory chapter and three subsequent parts. Part One discusses a number of illusions clustered around the parental roles assumed by the religious organization. Part Two continues the familial imagery which weaves itself throughout the book by viewing the church as a system with the same functional and dysfunctional processes found in most families. Part Three will help readers claim their own voices by assisting in the grieving of illusions; reconciling the accompanying, often crazy-making ambivalence; and transforming the illusions into viable images of faith.

PART ONE:
ILLUSIONS ABOUT RIGHTEOUS RELIGION

Chapter 1

Toward an Authentic Voice

There are uncounted numbers of people like the eight individuals in the Introduction who desire their Christianity to meet their spiritual needs on the deepest of levels. They yearn to be embraced and protected within their faith much like children trust parents to keep them safe.[1] Christians want their churches to be Christlike, providing not only for the hungry and the ill, but also for the wounded, the lonely, and the outcast. Also, believers come to church to be inspired by the word of God and the good news of God's love for them. They look to their congregation for comfort in times of sorrow and a nurturing presence through the perils of life. Further, the faithful need wisdom from their church and a guide to the Spirit living within them. Members return again and again to the stories of holy people who have gone before them and seek assurance that they also have a place in this saintly progression.

Many members of righteous religion require their churches to be philosophically reasonable, morally helpful, spiritually illuminating, and communally supportive.[2] In this regard, they look to their religion to validate the unconditional goodness of the human being and God's unconditional love for each. Christians earnestly wish for moral guidelines that are sufficiently flexible so as to be relevant to their life circumstances without distorting the underlying Christian principles. In other words, they want the church to help them become one with Christ within the contexts of their lives. Believers long for models of sacred lives with which they can identify, and for shaping stories broad enough to encompass their own human experiences. Finally, Christians want to be included in the community of faith and counted among God's children.

What a growing number of Catholics and Fundamentalists are

experiencing, however, are church structures that fail to meet their expectations and spiritual needs and may, in fact, even thwart them. For example, they are continually threatened with exclusion and eternal punishment at the hands of a parental angry God unless they abide by the dictates of righteous law and authority. Members encounter a belief-system that assumes that they are flawed and evil children and that only out of fear will they stay in line. In this regard, believers are terrified into obedience by frequent references to Satan, hell, and a final judgment presided over by a jealous and wrathful God.

Like a negative or conditional parent, authoritarian churches interpret law and scripture in a manner so absolute and rigid that mere mortals seldom can achieve the perfection demanded. This creates a situation where the children of faith often feel guilty for not measuring up and pleasing a perfect parent. Many Fundamentalists and Catholics are thus made to feel shameful and unworthy by constant reminders of their fallen and evil natures. This sense of being defective at their very core leaves them at the mercy of the dictates and leadership of righteous religion.

Many believers are feeling demoralized at having continually to fight demons lurking both within themselves and in the world at large. They are told that Satan is manifested in their thoughts, imaginations, daydreams, and passions and, keeping their emotions in check, their words monitored, and their bodies pure is an unrelenting struggle. Lest they lose this battle and eternal salvation, members are mandated to rely heavily on the authority of church leaders as they interpret either scripture (or, in the case of Catholics, tradition). Believers, therefore, often come to mistrust their own judgment, intuition, and spirit.

Therefore, Catholics and Fundamentalists hold one set of expectations about their churches, but often find a singularly different reality. On the one hand, they yearn for a godly home where they can find nurturance and comfort; an outreach to the downtrodden; moral guidance; and spiritual illumination. On the other hand, they encounter an authoritarian parent who threatens damnation and judgment; instills feelings of fear, guilt, and shame; and often renders them helpless and dependent.

When any of life's deepest hopes are grounded in illusions, children of all ages can experience disillusionment as their misplaced expectations about parents or the parental church are shattered. Their trust is betrayed when they experience threats and invalidation by either. They often feel disenchanted and disheartened when their best efforts to measure up to parental standards are somehow flawed or never good enough. Similarly, when their natural strivings to develop self-reliance in their relationship with God are discouraged, they fail to develop a sense of their own voices and, hence, an adult faith.

VOICE

"Voice is an indicator of self. Speaking one's feelings and thoughts is part of creating, maintaining, and recreating one's authentic self."[3] For faith to be truly adult and mature, it must reflect an individual's real self, rather than a self that is borrowed from the expectations of others. *Voice* in this book serves as a metaphor for being in communication with the soul or innermost being. Thus, having a voice involves the ability to express that deepest of connections with others and with God. To speak one's voice, then, is to reflect the voice of the Spirit within.

It would seem logical that the primary task of religion is to lay the groundwork for and nurture the spiritual voice of its members. Yet, what many believers are experiencing as they mature in their faith is a difficulty in accessing their deepest and most sacred selves. This dilemma is often a result of the church's conditional parenting, which frequently instills in its members a sense of inferiority and conflict. These painful feelings, combined with the parental church's expectation that its members censor and limit the range of their emotions, run counter to the emergence of an authentic voice in growing Christian children of all ages. Being conditioned to be dependent and compliant children, people form a pseudo or false self in order to preclude possible parental censure. People whose faith has components of fear, shame, unworthiness, and emotional restriction may have considerable difficulty developing the capacities for self-empowerment, individuation, self-esteem, independence, spontaneity, and trust in inner authority and Spirit that are the hallmarks of an authentic voice.

To be a good member of an authoritarian church is often to live with a divided self. One side is outwardly conforming and compliant, dutiful and faithful; whereas an inner, perhaps secret, side strives to express itself. Sometimes this inner self is enraged and resentful, at other times, sad and empty. There is a fundamental disconnection with the real, spiritual self and a burying and hiding of a sacred inner voice.[4] Chapter 4 ("Six Illusions of Religion as the Good Parent") will further elaborate on the conditional parenting of righteous religions and how this process results in many believers abdicating their voices. Such individuals become alienated from their spiritual intuition or from their own "ways of knowing."[5] They disbelieve the legitimacy of their own perspective, silence their convictions, and block creativity and imagination in an effort to comply with the church's parental voice.[6]

ILLUSIONS AND THE EMERGENCE
OF THE REAL SELF

Being raised under the conditional parenting of an authoritarian church structure, members feel the sword of exclusion and disapproval, both temporal and eternal, always hanging over their heads. Many believers, in order to deal with this threat and its accompanying loss, develop what James Masterson calls the false or pseudo self. This self can take two forms: becoming a helpless child, conforming to everyone else's wishes; or becoming an evil/bad child, constantly on the verge of rejection.[7] "In either case, the child fears that genuine self-expression will be punished with abandonment, and these two stances are designed to ward off that possibility. . . ."[8] Thus, many members, fearing potential abandonment by the parental church (and by inference, the parental God) unconsciously choose instead to abandon their real "selves" and silence their authentic voices. Thus, it is fairly easy to see why so many adherents of righteous religion assume one of these two roles, given how much of the language of their faith reinforces believers as either helpless and dependent children and/or evil creatures "constantly under the threat of divine punishment. . . ."[9]

Problems arise when compliant or supposedly bad Christian children begin to grow up and attempt to develop their own voices and identities. Often this growth process is initiated or accompanied by the crumbling of illusions about the parental church. In any case, dissonance is created when an emerging real and adult self runs counter to the false self that has been maintaining them in the illusory good graces of the church organization. Discordance ripples through the psyche of such growing individuals, and the pseudo self cracks open. Such people often feel vulnerable, helpless, confused, and betrayed by the authoritarian parental church which promised to keep them safe, affirmed, and guided through their lives.

In many ways, maturing believers can be seen as growing individuals in that their journey toward the real self has begun. No longer are they locked into the roles of the compliant or bad child but are now offered the opportunity to undertake the tasks of deconstructing and grieving illusions, reconciling ambivalences, and transforming spiritually. The closer people are to discovering their authentic voices, the freer and more capable they are of initiating these tasks.

Masterson lists some of the attributes of the real self[10] or what we refer to as an authentic voice:

- The capacity to experience a wide range of feelings deeply:
  - the ability to experience feelings in their truest form, without censoring or editing them.
- The capacity to expect entitlements:
  - the expectation of people that they have a right to master their lives and achieve what is good for them.
- The capacity for self-activation and assertion:
  - the ability to have individual dreams and goals and to pursue them actively and self-reliantly.
- The acknowledgment of self-esteem:
  - self recognition of worthwhileness, skills, and values.
- The ability to soothe painful feelings:
  - the capacity to access an internal source of comfort.
- The ability to make and stick to commitments:
  - the capacity, despite setbacks and obstacles, to follow through on pledges, promises, and undertakings.
- Creativity:
  - "the ability to replace old familiar patterns of living and problem-solving,"[11] with fresh and personally authentic ones.

- Intimacy:
  - "the capacity to express the real self fully and honestly in a close relationship with another person with minimal anxiety about abandonment or engulfment."[12]
- The ability to be alone:
  - the capacity to manage feelings without fear of abandonment when others are not present.
- Continuity of self:
  - the ability to apprehend a personal core that is eternal.

As believers shift from identifying with the pseudo self of the compliant child/bad child to attaining their real voices, an accompanying shift in their imagery for God occurs. As they begin to experience themselves as more authentic, more entitled to life in abundance, more hopeful, worthwhile, more self-nurturing, generative, and creative, they will naturally gravitate toward images of God that reflect their more radiant self.[13] Maturing individuals no longer need the restrictive ties to that which is punishing or fragmenting in the whitened sepulchers of righteous religion. Before any of this growth can occur, however, the outgrown childhood illusions regarding the church must be allowed to disintegrate and be grieved.

It is in the midst of the disillusionment felt by maturing believers that the ingredients for spiritual transformation are discovered. The growing pains of such individuals can be reframed as catalysts for reclaiming a basic trust in an unconditionally affirming and validating God and toward a life of increased generativity, purposefulness, hope, authenticity, creativity, imagination, and mystical faith.[14] It seems fairly well established in the adult developmental literature, however, that the path toward attaining an authentic voice expressive of the real self is often through disorientation and disillusionment.[15] Before Christians can find their voices and move beyond illusions, they must first step back from their expectations and assumptions about their churches and examine them objectively and realistically. Part One of this book offers that perspective in regard to erroneous notions about the authoritative and parental nature of church organizations, and Part Two looks at illusions in regard to these families of faith.

Chapter 2

Religion as the Fortress of Absolute Truth

Righteous religion impresses upon its members that it speaks with the voice of God and thus can be relied upon as a bastion of absolute truth. Throughout western European history, the boundaries between the Catholic church and God were blurred in the imagination of the believers, almost to the point that the two were merged into one reality. Thus, to obey the church was to obey God, to visit the church was to visit the place where God was truly present, to be forgiven by the church was to be forgiven by God, and to be blessed by the church was to be blessed by God. Very early in Christian history St. Cyprian set the tone for this illusory merging of God and Church when he wrote: "He cannot have God as his father, who does not have the Church as his mother."[1]

In the sixteenth century, Martin Luther challenged this merger between God and the church by contending that scripture and scripture alone was the source and basis for all Christian belief and practice. Church authority, then, derived its credibility from scripture. Luther's position was revolutionary in that, prior to this time, Judeo-Christian tradition had not understood scripture to stand on its own, independent from church authority. This former Augustinian friar initiated a major trend in Christendom and other Protestant reformers were quick to follow his lead.

There are undoubtedly numerous ways to examine the illusion of absolute truth in religion but this chapter will devote itself to two of the more predominant approaches. The following sections will provide discussions from both a Catholic and a Fundamentalist vantage point. After an overview of each perspective, the story of Margarite will illustrate illusions held by many devout Catholics. Conrad's story will describe the experience of many adherents of churches based on the Bible as the literal and inerrant word of God.

THE CATHOLIC CHURCH AS GOD

In examining their consciences before receiving the sacrament of Confession, pre-Vatican II Catholics were exhorted to ask themselves if they had doubted both their belief in God and their faith in the church, as if they were sins of the same magnitude.[2] While Catholics would quickly acknowledge that God was the source of forgiveness and remission of sins, they were firmly taught that, "the Church can remit temporal punishment due to sin with *Indulgences*, . . . provided the conditions which the Church imposes are fulfilled."[3]

Over the years, Catholics have been immersed in the God/church illusion with instructions that, "to hear the teachings of the Church and to submit oneself to its laws, is to hear Jesus Christ and to obey Him. To refuse to submit to the decisions and laws of the Church is to refuse to submit to Jesus Christ."[4] If Catholics needed to know what constituted God's truth, they were instructed to turn to the church, for what it "teaches comes from God, source of all truth. She hands down to us what God has revealed and that which has been taught and believed in the Church from its beginning."[5]

Thus, the eternal quest for God's will has led Catholics no further than the church. While rendering due reverence to sacred scripture as a source for ascertaining God's will, the church unhesitantly proclaimed that God's voice was most clearly heard when spoken through itself.[6]

Even with the updating of the Second Vatican Council, Catholics were exhorted to turn to the church, as they would to God, for truth and direction: "Like all Christians, the laity should promptly accept in Christian obedience what is decided by the pastors who, as teachers and rulers of the Church, represent Christ."[7] This interchangeability between God and church continues to be supported up to the present day by frequent references to the church as the spokesperson, representative, or sole agent for God on earth. Each Easter Sunday, Catholics renew their baptismal promises by vowing "to serve God faithfully in his Catholic Church."[8]

The *Catechism of the Catholic Church*, published in 1994, a statement of Catholic faith and doctrine, provides many examples of this God/church merger, insofar as the church acts in the place of God. For example, the *Catechism* contends that:

> Were there no forgiveness of sins in the Church, there would be no hope of life to come or eternal liberation. Let us thank God who has given his Church such a gift.[9]

Furthermore, according to *The Roman Catechism*, which is also supported by the current Catholic hierarchy, any attempt on the part of a sinner to seek reconciliation or reunification with God is useless because the Roman Catholic Church possesses the only keys to heaven's door through which a sinner may pass: "No one, therefore, can get into heaven unless it is opened to him by the priests to whose custody the keys have been given."[10]

In a 1990 Vatican declaration, little room is offered to Catholic theologians (not to mention Catholic laity) as to who speaks for God: "Within the particular churches, it is the bishop's responsibility to guard and interpret the Word of God and to make authoritative judgments as to what is or is not in conformity with it."[11] Thus, the church in arrogating to itself the role of sole interpreter of God's Word becomes virtually interchangeable with God in the minds of many Catholics. The church, by superimposing itself on the already intertwined imagery for God and parents, reinforces deep in the intellectual and affective beings of Catholics the illusion that God and the church are nearly one and the same.

The Story of Margarite

When Margarite was a little girl, the reality of the church and the concept of God were locked into her imagination as one entity. She fervently believed that St. Anne's was God's house and when Father McCarthy spoke at Sunday Mass, God was speaking through him. Like most impressionable children, she took rules literally and those of the church were the words and will of God. Since she loved God, she was very careful to do everything that Father McCarthy and Sister Mary Martha told her to do, so that she would please God and join Him in heaven someday. On the night of her First Communion, she refused to take a bath lest she have to remove the scapular that was given her that morning. After all, Sister had impressed upon her the necessity of wearing the cloth neckpiece at all times so that she could help the "poor souls" in Purgatory be released into heaven sooner.

Margarite and her family strove to be good Catholics. They attended Mass each Sunday and on all the Holy Days of Obligation, partook of confession on the first Saturday of every month, refrained from eating meat on Friday, prayed before and after meals, and recited the Rosary as a family every evening before bedtime. She never saw her father drive by a Catholic church without uttering a silent prayer and signing himself. Her family was such a model for other Catholics that her mother was designated St. Anne's Mother of the Year and Margarite herself won the religion award both in grade school and high school.

When she came of marriageable age, she was very careful to date only young Catholic men. She finally chose Robert, who, like herself, was a product of Catholic schools and was raised to believe and practice all that Holy Mother Church taught. Margarite was proud to be able to wear a white dress at her wedding, signifying that she had saved herself for Robert on their wedding night. She and Robert's marital encounters were open to the procreation of children as commanded by God and the church. It was only after the first five children arrived a year apart that they sought the advice of Father McCarthy's successor as to whether their circumstances justified practicing the church-sanctioned rhythm method of birth control.

It was over this very issue that differences began to surface between Robert and Margarite. The infrequency of their sexual encounters was upsetting to Robert who felt he deserved to unwind at night with Margarite. After all, he worked two jobs to support the seven of them, came home to a noisy house filled with children, and needed what he called an "outlet." Only once did Margarite give in, and nine months later, a daughter was born. After that, she vowed never to take chances again. Robert disagreed with the church's stand on birth control and was argumentative when she refused to deviate from the teachings of the Holy Father. After awhile, he stopped asking her to have sex even during the "safe" times.

During the years of the children's upbringing, Margarite raised them as she had been taught by the church. Each child was baptized at the proper time, went to confession, received First Communion, and was confirmed. The family never missed Mass at the required times and the children were instructed in the recitation of the Rosary and nightly prayers. Until the church changed the rules on abstaining from meat on Friday, they all adhered to that practice as well. Margarite saw to it that several Catholic periodicals as well as the diocesan newspaper were always present in their home. Further, she did everything possible to ensure salvation for herself and her family. She even recited a daily decade of the rosary for Robert who had grown emotionally distant from her.

After the children left home, Margarite devoted much of her free time to serving God by serving His church. She taught catechism each Monday and Wednesday to grade school children, was active in the altar society, and helped prepare meals after each parish funeral. As the abortion issue came to greater prominence, she joined St. Anne's Right to Life Committee and marched with them in front of the local abortion clinic on Saturday afternoon. Margarite was seen by nearly everyone at her church as a pillar of the parish. She always responded when priests asked her to give time to special projects and she was considered the epitome of Catholic womanhood.

Beneath the facade of Margarite's ideal Christian family, however, all was not well. One morning as she was leaving for Mass, Harriet, her next door neighbor, asked her if she had a redheaded daughter. When Margarite said no, Harriet related how her own husband had seen Robert in the company of a young redhead, last weekend in a nearby city. Suddenly, the puzzling pieces fell together for Margarite. She now knew why Robert had been so distant and preoccupied over the years and why business frequently kept him out of town or working late at the office. Rather than confront Robert, Margarite chose, like the Holy Mother of God, to keep this matter locked secretly in her heart.

If this wasn't painful enough, her own children were beginning to stray from the mandates of Catholicism, thus placing their salvation in jeopardy. Several of them seemed to be making up their own rules rather than abiding by the will of God as expressed by church teaching. For example, she was well aware that two of her daughters practiced artificial contraception and neither expressed any guilt when Margarite confronted them. She was surprised and ashamed when she felt jealous of her daughters. They had so much more freedom and ability to control their lives than she had at their age; and additionally, her daughters could enjoy relations with their husbands without fear of pregnancy driving them into the arms of a redheaded woman. When Margarite became aware of the envy in which she was indulging and the extent to which she was entertaining un-Christian and lustful thoughts, she was mortified. Even though she had made her monthly confession two weeks previously, she phoned the rectory to make an appointment for confession that very day. She was conscience-stricken and felt an urgent need to return to God's good grace by means of the church's anointed representatives at St. Anne's.

Margarite was still feeling the sting of disappointment concerning her two daughters' refusal to abide by the church's sanctions on birth control when she received news about two of her other children. When her son Luke informed her of his imminent divorce, she felt consumed with guilt. Luke was the only one of their six children not to graduate from Catholic High School. "If only I hadn't allowed him to transfer to South High after his freshman year," she repeated to herself over and over again. She was convinced that she had failed to provide him with a sufficiently firm foundation of faith upon which to ground a lifelong Christian marriage.

During the same week, her youngest child, Catherine, told her that she was lesbian. Margarite's remorse intensified. This was the child that she had reluctantly conceived. Margarite was convinced that it was due to her lack of openness to procreation that Catherine had turned her back on the Lord's natural order and chosen this sinful life-style. Both mother and daughter had defied God's word as promulgated by the church and were now suffering the consequences.

Margarite prayed ceaselessly for the salvation of four of her six children and pleaded with God at daily Mass to have mercy upon her failure as a parent. She thought of Jesus Christ and the crushing cross he had to bear and reminded herself that no cross was too heavy for her to carry.

To many, Margarite can be viewed as the perfect Catholic. She faithfully obeyed all the rules and commandments enjoined upon her by the church and took each mandate to be an expectation of God himself. In this regard, Margarite's illusion that God and the church were merged into one contributed to much of her distress. Had she not held this illusion, she may have heard God speaking in many other ways in her life. As it was, she accepted the Spirit only as described and defined by the church. Since she conceived God in such a singular and narrow manner, she was unable to respond in anything but a similarly constricted and rigid style. By substituting the voice of the church for her own voice, Margarite was unable to relate to God in a fashion authentic to her true self.

FUNDAMENTALISM AND THE VOICE OF GOD

As discussed previously regarding Protestant Bible-based traditions, the equation between church and God is represented by the merging of scripture and God. The Bible is the one and final authority for practice and belief, and sacred scripture constitutes an inerrant source of inspiration. Believers within these traditions hold to the view that God communicated directly either in biblical revelation or biblical inspiration. Thus to know God's will, they need go no further than the Bible.

Adherents of Bible-based churches maintain that "all Scripture is God-breathed and is useful for teaching, rebuking, correcting, and training in righteousness (2 Timothy 3:16)."[12] The proof that the Bible is literally God's word is supported by the fact that the Lord told Jeremiah to take a scroll and have written on it all the words that God wished to reveal (Jeremiah 36:1-2).[13] When believers hold that the Bible is God's word, there is, thus, the certainty that each word is inspired by God or dictated from Yahweh's mouth into the ear of a prophet or a scribe.

Fundamentalist churches teach that the Gospel is the power of God for the salvation of everyone who believes (Romans 1:16).[14] To be planted firmly in scripture is to be surrounded by the power of God and to hold to scripture is to be assured of salvation. The words that God has spoken through the prophets and in the "last days" (Hebrews 1:2)[15] through his son are the entirety of revelation. All that humans need to know of God's will and wisdom has been spoken and is contained in the Bible. Thus the biblical word is absolute, and its statements are inerrant and unchanging for peoples of different times and in all cultures.

While the Bible is the central authority for such churches, actual authority is often transferred to a minister, especially if he (seldom she) is an excellent preacher or presides over a large and growing congregation. For smaller flocks, power is frequently invested in elders and deacons. These ministers and elders exercise the responsibility for applying, interpreting, and proclaiming scripture. They also have been given gifts for preparing "God's people for works of service," building up the body of Christ, keeping the members from being "blown here and there by every wind of teaching," and holding them together (Ephesians 4:12-16).[16] A preacher particularly is considered by the flock to speak the word of God and is given through the Spirit the message of knowledge (1 Corinthians 12:3,8).[17] Like Paul the Apostle, ministers are called to become servants of the gospel and "to make plain to everyone the administration of this mystery" (Ephesians 3:7,9).[18] Accordingly, they believe that "through the church, the manifold wisdom of God should be made known to the rulers and authorities in the heavenly realms" (Ephesians 3:10).[19]

Members of Fundamentalist churches who submit to the authority of scripture as interpreted and proclaimed by their ministers and church authorities are unknowingly entertaining at least two illusions. The first illusion states that the will of God is contained and expressed once and for all time in a single book that must be read and lived literally. Faith, then, is grounded exclusively in this inerrant volume written nearly two thousand years ago in an agricultural region of the Middle East and at a time when knowledge of geography, science, and history was far more limited than today. A second illusion centers around the ministers and the churches over which they preside. For many believers in these preachers and institutions, human error is not possible in either the reading, interpretation, or proclaiming of God's word. Both consciously and unconsciously, members believe that representatives of God's kingdom are devoid of personal agendas, biases, or perceptual errors and distortions. Thus, they hear the words of preachers as the true and uncontaminated word of God and humbly and willingly submit to it.

The Story of Conrad

Conrad's life changed irrevocably when at age twelve he first met a preacher, Pastor Harold Jones, who had recently been called to minister at Victory Fellowship. Victory was a small and struggling congregation whose members had heard that this young preacher was a dynamic orator. Thus, the elders felt that he might be just the man to turn their mid-city church into a vital Bible center providing family-minded ministry.

Conrad's parents had been among the founders of Victory Fellowship and had dedicated him to God when Conrad was an infant. At age eight he had made a decision to accept Jesus as his personal Lord and Savior and had received Christ into his heart. The arrival of Pastor Jones, shortly after Conrad had been saved, further energized his faith and engendered in him new zeal for exalting God and evangelizing the lost. Through the youth ministry, personally led by Pastor Jones, Conrad became proficient in proclaiming the Gospel of Jesus Christ. As a result of Conrad's dedicated ministry, many young people were brought forward to choose Jesus and be born again. His efforts, combined with the inspirational preaching of Pastor Jones, necessitated Victory Fellowship expanding its facilities and ministries and proudly proclaiming itself as a dynamic church of praise, worship, and the word.

Prior to his graduation from high school, Conrad sought Pastor Jones' help in obtaining admission to the Bible college where Pastor Jones had excelled several years previously. Conrad wanted to pursue his business degree in an atmosphere where the uncompromised word of faith was taught in truth and fellowship. Shortly after arriving he met Susan who, like himself, had been saved and thus shared his values. They fell in love and married the summer before their sophomore year. Finances were difficult and, since both believed that the husband was head of the wife, they decided that Susan would withdraw from college and work to support them while Conrad completed his education.

The Lord blessed them with their first child on Conrad's graduation day. They named their son Harold. Two daughters were born in succeeding years. All three offspring were brought up "in the training and instruction of the Lord" (Ephesians 6:4).[20] The children were faithfully taken to Sunday morning worship service and Sunday School, Sunday night celebration of praise, and Wednesday evening family night. Once the girls were in junior high and Harold in high school, Susan decided she wanted to finish college and become an elementary school teacher.

As head of the household, Conrad was reluctant to give her permission to attend the local state university. He frequently quoted to her the words of Romans 16, instructing her to keep away from people who are not serving our Lord Jesus. He admonished her that "by smooth talk and flattery they deceive the minds of naive people" (Romans 16:18).[21] Being a good wife, she silenced her anger at being called "naive" but, for the first time in their marriage, chose not to submit to his authority.

At college Susan was required to take a series of general education courses where the eyes of her mind were gradually opened to new and challenging perspectives. She enjoyed eating lunch with other reentry students, people who, like herself, came from diverse backgrounds. Up to this time, she had socialized only with women from Victory Fellowship, and these new friends offered her points of view and ideas that she had never considered. It was in such gatherings and in her classes that she learned about the validity of other religions and an alternative way of perceiving the evolution of the species. She also discovered that many so-called feminists were not evil companions, but were women like herself who were seeking an education and an equal opportunity for advancement. Susan felt torn. At college she was invigorated, genuinely happy, and free for the first time in her adult life. At home she felt constricted and caught between her increasingly different worlds.

Conrad perceived that something was changing in Susan and in their relationship. He was convinced Satan was at work in his household and he set about questioning her about possible errors in the teaching she was receiving at what he called "that pagan college." It all came to a head one Sunday night when Susan declined to attend the evening celebration of praise due to a test the next day. After delivering a barrage of Scripture quotes dealing with the fires of hell, Conrad finally ordered her to submit to his authority and accompany him to the church service. Susan not only refused but informed him of her doubts about literal interpretation of scripture, the objective reality of hell, creationism, and the subordinate status of women.

Their son Harold chose this time to tell Conrad that he too wasn't going to the evening service since, like his mother, he had exams the next day. He also told his father that he didn't see what the big deal was about going to celebration on Sunday nights since he had been to worship service that morning. Conrad strove to contain his anger and attempted to follow Paul's instruction for husbands and fathers not to be harsh and bitter. He then read to them from 2 Timothy (3:26) about their pride, disobedience, lack of gratitude, conceit, and unholiness. He warned them about evil influences and how they "worm their way into homes and gain control over weak-willed women."[22] Conrad's words only strengthened Susan's resolve and she informed him that she and Harold had to be about their Father's business, which in this case was their studies. With that, Conrad gathered up his daughters for the celebration service and, as he left, quoted Luke 11:17 that "a house divided against itself will fall."[23]

Frustrated at home, Conrad decided to devote himself to Pastor Harold's new crusade to evangelize the many unsaved souls in their city. He spent most of his free hours raising money for the crusade, and, due to his accounting expertise, was named Chairman of Finance. In this new ministry, he became involved with reaching out to the lost and bringing them to accept the Lord. Because of his outreach work, he became increasingly concerned about Susan and young Harold's salvation. He went so far as to have a team of elders visit them at home in an attempt to snatch them from Satan's grip lest their souls be doomed.

While working closely with Pastor Harold, Conrad began to glimpse a different side to this servant of God whom he so admired. Some of those involved in the crusade were giving evidence of resisting the pastor's authority over financial issues. They felt that the crusade was focusing more on money than on salvation and they wanted an accounting of his stewardship. One day, Conrad was shocked as he watched his minister and spiritual mentor explode into a wrathful and ungodly tirade on the crusade's godly people. The pastor hurled Scripture at them and finally rebuked them with Romans 13:2, "he who rebels against the authority is rebelling against what God has instituted, and those who do so will bring judgment on themselves."[24]

Pastor Harold's outburst set Conrad questioning his trust in his minister. Conrad quietly reviewed the accounts and noticed that significant funds were missing. This forced him to reflect on what he had always considered to be his pastor's well-deserved lifestyle–his elegant wife, wonderful home, and top-of-the-line automobile. Conrad chose to push all this out of his mind and remained focused on his ministry to lost souls. His faith and his work at Victory Fellowship were central to his life, especially now since Susan and Harold seemed to be slipping into the hands of the infidel. It gave him some sense of satisfaction to know that he was still able to influence his daughters toward salvation.

Much like Margarite in the previous story, Conrad viewed his religion as a fortress of absolute truth. Whereas Margarite gave herself over to the teaching authority of the Catholic church, Conrad submitted to the authority of scripture as proclaimed by Pastor Harold and the elders at Victory Fellowship. Conrad's faith was based on the twofold illusions of biblical inerrancy and the righteousness of those who preach in the name of the Lord Jesus. During the course of events described in this story, both of these illusions were challenged, although neither shattered. If Conrad's perception of scripture had been broader, he might have been able to hear Susan's views and approach the family dissension in a more conciliatory and tolerant manner. Similarly, had he not so unequivocally equated the word of God with its minister, he might have been able to access his own inner authority and act with more responsibility toward the possible theft of church funds. As it was, Conrad's illusions allowed him to surrender his own voice of truth to external authority and prevented him from hearing God's voice within him.

Chapter 3

Religion as a Parent

Margarite and Conrad had been taught that God spoke through their churches. Since God for them was framed in Father-like terms, they had come to expect numerous parental functions from their church. With the parental God seemingly at a distance in heaven, religiously bonded people, such as Conrad and Margarite, need an earthly parent closer to themselves. Thus, following the tradition of the Apostle Paul (1 Corinthians 4:14-15), the church and its stewards have been assigned (or assigned to themselves) many of the features of the distant Father with the members assuming the role of children.[1] For these children of faith, church serves as a protector in times of trouble, a provider of their needs, a comforter, an educator/guide, and a repository for family history.

PROTECTOR

Just as parents see themselves as a buffer between their offspring and all that may potentially endanger them, so righteous religion defines itself as the guardian or protector from all that could harm its children. Human parents look after the safety of their children so that they may live a long and happy life. Likewise, some churches are vigilant over members so as to preserve their souls for everlasting life with God. Mothers and fathers guard against such dangers as physical harm, diseases, and bad companions. Churches are sworn to keep their members safe from the wages of sin and evil influences that could lead their children to the eternal fires of hell.

In this regard, Catholics are encouraged to cling to the church for external salvation and the church, in turn, promises to embrace them "within the bosom of her love."[2] This protective embrace is often provided by the church's leaders who are never to leave the flock untended and to watch over it and protect it always.[3] Likewise, Catholics are cared for by the Virgin Mother of God under "whose protection the faithful take refuge together in prayer in all their perils and needs."[4] Similarly, both Catholics and Fundamentalists are admonished to obey their leaders and submit to their authority for "they keep watch over you as men who must give an account" (Hebrews 13:17).[5]

A metaphor that bolsters and demonstrates religion's protective stance toward the faithful is that of shepherd and flock. Leaders take their cue from Paul who encourages them to keep watch over "all the flock of which the Holy Spirit has made you overseers. Be shepherds of the church of God, which he bought with his own blood" (Acts 20:28).[6] Employing this imagery, the Catholic Church describes itself as a "sheepfold, the sole and necessary gateway to which is Christ."[7] The bishop is frequently described as a shepherd in "the permanent and daily care of . . . sheep" and he is admonished not to "refuse to listen to his subjects whose welfare he promotes as of his very own children. . . ."[8]

PROVIDER

Mothers and fathers assume responsibility for supplying food, shelter, medical care, and clothing for their offspring. A church, in a similar manner, provides spiritual care and nourishment for its children. Thus, members of parental religions have the right to receive spiritual sustenance from their churches, which might include the word of God or the sacraments. Just as biological parents try to meet the material needs of their children, so religious leaders provide the spiritual conditions that will enable the Son of God to grant them entrance into eternal life (John 3:16).[9] As such, then, authoritarian religions help members to put on the full armor of God so that they can take their "stand against the devil's schemes" (Ephesians 6:11).[10]

Like a parent, the Christian church throughout history has provided material care for her children in need. It furnished shelter for travelers or pilgrims, food for the hungry, sanctuary for the alien, clothing for the naked, and medical care for the ill. Religious orders, missionary societies, and agencies arose for the purpose of offering these services. Stories of those who heroically performed works of Christian charity have circulated widely among believers and succeeded in reinforcing the notion of the church as a providential parent.

The clearest example of spiritual nourishment is found in Catholicism's understanding of communion, wherein Christ is made present in the form of bread and wine. In the minds of many Catholics, Jesus' presence is found in the familial setting of a sup-per-like service and the homey imagery of daily bread fed to them by the priest or eucharistic minister. Communion is the spiritual food which sustains them on their pilgrimage through life and is available only through their religion. Both Catholics and Funda-mentalists, however, believe that by partaking in Communion, that is by eating the body of Christ and drinking his blood, they share in Jesus' life (1 Corinthians 10:16) and proclaim his death until he comes again (1 Corinthians 11:26).[11]

COMFORTER

Comforting in the sense of consoling, reassuring, or lightening the burdens of one's children is seen by parental churches as a viable part of their mission. The first letter to the Thessalonians provides a model for such nurturing behavior when Paul describes himself as a father dealing with his own children, "encouraging, comforting, and urging you to live lives worthy of God" (Thessalonians 2:11-12).[12] Many parental churches might reecho the Catholic Church's self-definition as a holy mother, who "encompasses with her love all those who are afflicted by human misery and she recognizes in those who are poor and who suffer, the image of her poor and suffering founder. She does all in her power to relieve their need and in them she strives to serve Christ."[13] This maternal imagery is reinforced by the words of Isaiah, in which God is seen to be a mother comforting her child (Isaiah 66:13).[14] God is the source of all comfort (Isaiah 49:23) and, as the Father of compassion, comforts his people in all their troubles. In turn, they, and by extension their communities of faith, can comfort others (2 Corinthians 1:4; 7:6-7).[15]

For the most part, however, the nurturing aspect of religion with which most believers are familiar is there to help them avoid the perils of sin, deal with the sorrow of death, and face the impending encounter with God. Within this context, Christians often hope that a representative of the church will nurture them through their guilt and shame and help them face God at the judgment seat (Romans 14:10).[16] An image for many believers is that of a prayerful priest, minister, or church representative attentively present at a dying person's bedside and comforting the family afterward. The nurturing that the church supplies in this instance is the ability to counteract the sense of terror caused by expiring individuals' fear of the devil, who is like a roaring lion, ready to devour them at the moment of death (1 Peter 5:8).[17] Thus, in this and in the broader context, the comforting of the parent-like church is almost always directed toward the sinful, sorrowing, or dying child.

EDUCATOR/GUIDE

A primary role that parents assume for their children is that of teacher. In this regard, parents help form their children's environment, transmit information about life, teach survival skills, and assist them in discriminating right from wrong, safety from danger, and good from bad. Additionally, they act as lawgivers and disciplinarians when the laws are transgressed.

The similarity between these parental roles and the teaching role religion has occupied in the lives of most Christians is striking. In fact, the Catholic church has defined itself as a mother who is under an obligation "to provide for . . . children an education by virtue of which their whole lives may be inspired by the spirit of Christ."[18] By the same token, many leaders of Fundamentalist churches follow Paul's example by instructing members "how to live in order to please God" (1 Thessalonians 4:1).[19] "The elders who direct the affairs of the church well are worthy of double honor, especially those whose work is preaching and teaching" (1 Timothy 5:17).[20] In this respect, clergy are to proclaim the word of God in its fullness, admonish and teach in all wisdom, and discern when the believers require milk or are mature enough in faith to receive solid food. In other words such teachers are to provide the elementary truths of

God's word, teach about righteousness, and train members to distinguish good from evil (Colossians 1:25,28; Hebrews 5:11-14).[21]

While most human mothers and fathers are somewhat insecure in their parenting, the parental style of righteous religion exhibits no such uncertainty. Pointing to Christ's words in Matthew, many priests and ministers are certain that what they bind on earth by way of laws and morality is bound in heaven (Matthew 16:19).[22] In fact, the Catholic Church proclaims that "Christ endowed the Church's shepherds with the charism of infallibility in matters of faith and morals,"[23] and considers "the refusal to believe all that the holy Church our Mother proposes to our faith" to be the sin of heresy.[24]

Most members of authoritarian religions experience parental teaching from Sunday Schools, Vacation Bible Schools, or religious education programs. In many ways, the instruction offered influences nearly all aspects of their lives. They are taught to keep occupied with work or play; to resist the sources of sin within themselves; and to avoid unsavory companions, dirty magazines, and bad movies (or in some cases, all movies). They are charged to be vigilant about such matters as superstition, uncharitable or boastful or bragging speech, punk rock, dancing, "getting even," soap operas, drinking and smoking, saying "gosh darn," *Mad* magazine, and going "too far" on dates.[25] They are instructed to safeguard their faith by studying their religion, attending Sunday School, living a good life, reading the Bible, and refusing to associate with nonbelievers. Christian boys and girls are often left with little doubt about the sinfulness of watching questionable television programs, shopping on Sunday, wearing dresses that don't cover enough, entertaining unchaste thoughts, and "touching one's own body or that of another without necessity simply to satisfy sinful curiosity."[26] And like many parents, righteous religions have instructions on what to eat, what to wear, what to say/when to say it/how to say it, what to think, and how and what to feel.

REPOSITORY OF HISTORY

Human parents often make an effort to pass on to their children a sense of where they came from, their place in the family history, and some idea of the traditions that have been handed down through preceding generations. Children see pictures of ancestors, hear stories about family heroes and heroines whom they can emulate, and are taught the domestic traditions and rituals of how to celebrate holidays and prepare certain meals.

The parental church does much the same thing. It retells the lives of the saints and Bible heroes such as David, Paul, and Esther, and, in doing so provides its children examples of how to obey God, how to be steadfast in keeping God's statutes, and how to patiently suffer torments and tortures for the faith. It presents a tableau of holy ancestors who constitute an "inheritance of the saints in the kingdom of light" (Colossians 1:12).[27] By fellowshipping with other children of God, believers participate in the ancient legacies of their faith (1 John).[28] Many of the traditions and rituals of the church, like those of the family, have evolved over time. Some of the rites and prayers are as old as Christianity itself, and all serve to assist members with passages throughout life and to provide hope for the future.

By preserving its history and faithfully retelling it, parental churches provide evidence of their endurance and stability. Like parents relating family stories to their children, religion helps members appreciate their place in the continuity of a community that has been promised to last until the end of the age (Matthew 28:18-20).[29] Likewise, the reading of Scripture during worship services treats its listeners to formative mythology and shaping stories so they may gain perspective for their own lives. An example of one of these liberating themes is taken from the book of Exodus (14) wherein the chosen people's miraculous passage through the Red Sea is an image of God's children being saved through the waters of baptism.[30]

SUMMARY

Whereas both Fundamentalism and Catholicism purport to facilitate a relationship between God and believers, in actuality they derive much of their authority from representing the parental God on earth. In the face of what often feels like a distant and intangible parent-like God, people desire to be held and surrounded by a closer and more defined "fatherly" presence. Likewise, with the will and word of God able to be construed so differently, they yearn for a source of parental certitude. Religions such as Bible-based Christianity and Catholicism have traditionally met these needs by assuming many of the roles and functions of the heavenly and sometimes inaccessible parent. The tradeoff in this process is that by satisfying people's needs, such religions often end up usurping the voices of many believers. The result is that religiously bonded individuals may speak with their church's voice and not their own.

Chapter 4

Six Illusions of Religion
as the Good Parent

By virtue of the authoritarian and parental roles of protector, provider, comforter, educator, and repository of history, a certain connection between the church and the parent is established in the psyche of believers. For many, then, the church is as influential in terms of their genetic heritage as their birth parents since the parental imprinting of their religion is so profound that it virtually becomes a part of their very blood. Because of this imprinting, members of authoritarian religions come to expect their churches to fulfill many functions similar to those of parents (preferably good parents).

But, is the church really a "good enough" parent or is this an illusion? Does authoritarian and righteous religion truly accept children unconditionally or are there qualifiers to their inclusion? Rather than operating out of a context of positive modeling, can it be said that such religions tend to parent by inducing fear and guilt in their members? Instead of promoting a healthy, viable sense of self, do these parental churches imprint a shameful, unworthy, or even false self-image? Do such religions help their children deal authentically with feelings, or do they often ask believers to invalidate their true emotions and stifle their voices? Finally, while good parents provide their children with the resources for independent living, does authoritarian religion frequently create a condition of dependency whereby its adult children are not able to trust their own truth and the voice of the Spirit deep within themselves? This chapter will discuss these six illusions of righteous religion as the good parent.

INCLUSION/EXCLUSION?

Children of "good enough" parents know with some certainty that their parents will always include them regardless of the circumstances. Granted, such parents must set limits on certain behaviors and mete out consequences, but loving parents will never banish their children forever from their presence or otherwise create conditions that may lead to feelings of alienation. This does not seem to be the case for God as portrayed in much of righteous religion, in which the frequent biblical references to God's saving some and punishing others are preached from pulpits. While Fundamentalism generally teaches that salvation is secure once people have received Christ and been born again, the messages they hear often seem to contradict this. Rather than being assured that once they are saved, they are always saved, they are told to submit to the commands, degrees, and stipulations of God as interpreted by the leaders of these churches. Failure to do so will arouse the displeasure of a jealous God whose anger will burn against them and will destroy them from the face of the land (Deuteronomy 6:15-16).[1]

Some clergy seem to have inside information as to whom God will consign to "the eternal fire prepared for the devil and his angels" (Matthew 25:41),[2] and consider it their primary task to exhort the faithful to be among the righteous who are destined for eternal life (Matthew 25:46).[3] Punishment and blazing fire are promised to unbelievers "who do not know God and do not obey the gospel of our Lord Jesus" (2 Thessalonians 1:7-8).[4] Of course, what constitutes both the gospel of Jesus and the rules of obedience are carefully dictated by authoritarian religions and those who fail to heed such dictates "will be shut out from the presence of the Lord" (2 Thessalonians 1:9).[5] "Truth" is of central importance for these righteous religions and is dispensed as infallible doctrine, gospel values, or authentic and consistent teaching. Those who refuse to love and abide by such truths become the playthings of Satan and will surely perish under the sentence of everlasting destruction and exclusion from the Lord's presence (2 Thessalonians).[6]

The destination for all this fury and eternal damnation is hell, where anyone who follows Satan, rather that obeying religious leaders, will be destroyed.[7] For authoritarian religions, the doctrine of hell is essential and great effort is made to ensure that believers take hell seriously.[8] J. I. Packer, a professor of theology, in summarizing the scriptural references for hell, describes it as a place of incineration, fire and darkness, weeping and grinding of truth, destruction and torment–all of which are unending. Moreover, hell is where God unleashes displeasure, righteous condemnation, and anger like a consuming fire upon those who have been defiant and who cling to the sins that God loathes.[9] Professor Packer ends his biblically inspired treatise on hell with two thoughts: "Those who are in hell will know not only that for their doings they deserve it but also that in their hearts they chose it;" and "It is really a mercy to mankind that God in Scripture is so explicit about hell. We cannot now say that we have not been warned."[10]

Unlike born-again Christians who get no second chances after death to achieve redemption, Catholics believe that in that vast void between earthly life and the eternal reaches of heaven and hell, there lies "a place or state of purification"[11] known as purgatory. Many Catholics are conditioned by the parental church to be solicitous for the eternal welfare of their loved ones, since their inclusion into heaven remains in doubt. On the one hand, they are told that those "in purgatory are at peace because they know that they are destined to be united to God in heaven."[12] On the other hand, there is still that lingering doubt as to whether their loved ones indeed will be liberated from the fire of purgatory or if they are among those who are dead in mortal sin and "derive little advantage from the prayers and supplications of others."[13] Thus, grieving Catholics are often forced into an agonizing position of having to beg and plead with a supposedly compassionate Father for the welfare of their own departed mothers, fathers, sisters, and brothers.

Equally disconcerting to many Christians is the role that Christ plays in regard to their acceptability. Believers sometimes are left with the impression that Jesus' friendship with men and women is conditional, depending upon the presence or absence of sin in their souls (Matthew 25:31-46; James 2:14-26).[14] Further, the supposedly gentle and welcoming Jesus is cast in the disconcerting role of sitting at the right hand of the Father, judging the living and the dead (Matthew 13:40-43; John 5:22-30; Acts 10:42),[15] and determining either their exclusion or inclusion into the eternal presence of their Father.

Most Christians are trained from an early age that they must guard themselves from a plethora of sins. Whether these sins are described as mortal or venial, little sins or big sins, they are still sins. "God hates sin. Period. Big sins, little sins; horrible, ghastly sins, or 'little white lies.' God hates them all because they separate you from him and, if they are not cleansed, hold the potential to plunge you into hell."[16] Catholics specifically believe that should death come upon individuals and sin be found in their souls, then they will be cut off from God's grace and enter hell.[17] In any case, the threat of hell is constantly held over the heads of members of righteous religion. For many, there is a lurking uncertainty as to whether their eternal salvation is assured, and this makes them continually apprehensive about where they stand with the parental God and whether their place with that God is ever a sure thing. Protestants in authoritarian religion are told that ". . . God doesn't always pour out immediate punishment for sin, but he always judges sin. No sinner goes unnoticed . . . Judgment is certain. It will come, maybe not today, perhaps not tomorrow, but it will come."[18] For Catholics, the situation is equally precarious since the church teaches that dead, unbaptized infants can only "hope" for God's infinite mercy,[19] while babies who are baptized before death are already in God's kingdom.[20] If the parental church can cast doubt about the inclusion of newborn infants, it's no wonder that adult Catholics have doubts about whether they will ever measure up to the conditional parent's expectations.

The issue of inclusion/exclusion pertains not only to the life beyond, but also has relevance for who is in or out in the temporal world. For example, according to *The Roman Catechism*, (which has been described in the *Catechism of the Catholic Church* as "a work of the first rank as a summary of Christian teaching") in the household of the Catholic Church infidels and the excommunicated are out, while heretics and schismatics "are liable to have judgment passed on their opinions, to be visited with spiritual punishments, and to be denounced with anathema."[21] Also out are "those who disregard their legitimate pastors, the bishops and priests, and thus separate themselves from the Holy Roman Church."[22]

Not to be outdone by the Catholics, Southern Baptists have totaled up the potentially doomed souls and the "unsaved" in precise percentages. Employing a secret formula, the Home Mission Board of the church estimated that, in 1993, 46.1 percent of people in Alabama risked going to hell since they hadn't been born again and accepted Jesus as their personal savior. This accounting of the potentially doomed apparently included significant numbers of Catholics as well as Jews, Hindus, Buddhists, and virtually all members of other non-Christian religions.[23] The Southern Baptists' penchant for lists of the unwashed seems to have originated with the Apostle Paul who warns the Corinthians not to associate with believers who are sexually immoral or with the greedy or swindlers or idolaters or drunkards or slanderers. True Christians were to hand such believers over to Satan so that their sinful nature may be destroyed. Further, Paul advises his readers to expel the wicked from the midst of the righteous (1 Corinthians 5:5-13).[24]

FEAR

Parents of small children often need to oversimplify the consequences of acts because of the child's limited level of understanding. But as offspring grow, "good enough" parents develop a certain degree of trust in their children's ability to make wise and ethical decisions. Authoritarian parents assume a distrustful stance and treat their maturing sons and daughters not only as mischievous toddlers, but also as if they were defective, incompetent, and morally flawed. Because parents don't trust their little ones, they often try to scare them into behaving.

The worst fear for humans is that of being emotionally orphaned or abandoned by those whom they love or upon whom they depend. The parental church seems to play on this primordial, deep-seated fear by its constant threat of separation from the loving Father. Members are taught that "the wages of sin is death" and that, unless they become "slaves to righteousness," they will surely die (Romans 6:15-23).[25] Thus some Christians live with the fear that they have neither hated sin above all things, nor have loved God enough, nor have sacrificed their lives sufficiently to prevent the forfeiture of God's grace.

The fear of being ensnared by the devil has been pervasive in the upbringing of most members of righteous religions. The devil, or

Satan, personifies all that these Christians have been taught to fear or avoid. This malevolent figure is described as the father of lies (John 8:44)[26] and his dirty work is first seen when, taking the guise of a serpent, he tempted Eve in the Garden of Eden, thus catapulting all humanity into a state of sinful depravity (Genesis 6:5).[27] Satan, the enemy, "prowls around like a roaring lion looking for someone to devour" (1 Peter 5:8).[28] For believers, then, the devil is the infernally cunning, cruel, and sinister bogeyman, constantly trying to outwit and lead believers away from God and toward a life of death-dealing sin. Satan "knows if he can get you to let down the defenses of your mind it won't be long before he wraps his red-hot fingers around your heart."[29]

And Satan doesn't work alone. He surrounds himself with a hostile host of demons (Matthew 12:24-28) whom he dispatches to various locations around the world.[30] Citing Revelation 12:4, many who interpret the Bible literally believe that when Satan swept his tail, a third of the stars of heaven were flung to earth, thus indicating the enormous number of demons let loose upon humanity.[31] Authoritarian churches utilize demonic imagery as a means of terrifying believers into obeying the moral standards, precepts, and teachings of their religion. Words such as "constant vigilance" and "spiritual warfare" are used to describe the stance that committed Christians are to assume against a malignant enemy who is unrelentingly laying snares for them.

If Satan is not enough to scare the wavering into submission, the punishments meted out by God upon sinners are graphically described in order to lead them toward righteousness. Righteous religion often will highlight a wrathful God (Romans 1:18; Ephesians 5:6) who condemns those who are disobedient (Romans 6:18)[32], and punishes all who do not control their own bodies or who cheat others (1 Thessalonians 4:6).[33] God, according to such religions, sides with the righteous (i.e., those who obey the commands of their religious leaders) and will pay back with trouble those who trouble such holy individuals. This God will punish with everlasting destruction those who do not know him and "shut out from the presence of the Lord" those who do not obey the gospel of Jesus Christ (2 Thessalonians 1:6-9).[34] If this image of God is not sufficient to keep people in line, ministers might quote Deuteronomy 6:15, in which God is described as a jealous God, whose anger burns against sinners and destroys them from the face of the land.[35] This anger and wrath will send enemies to the godless and these adversaries will "trample them down like mud in the streets" (Isaiah 10:5-7).[36]

Playing on the fears of its members, some churches endeavor to keep the faithful on the narrow path of virtue by holding over their heads the horrifying prospect of final judgment. At this event,

> In the presence of Christ . . . the truth of each man's relationship with God will be laid bare. The Last Judgment will reveal even to its furthest consequences the good each person has done or failed to do during his earthly life. . . . The message of the Last Judgment calls men to conversion while God is still giving them "the acceptable time, . . . the day of salvation."[37]

To alleviate the fearful consequences of their human conditions, Catholics are given the opportunity to confess their sins to a priest. They are warned, however, that should they relapse into the same sin after having it absolved in Confession, "their condition will be made much worse than before their conversion to God." Against those newly absolved from sin, "the enemy of mankind [sic] employs all his deceits and exerts all his powers," assailing "them with such violence as to justify the fear that they may waver in their good resolutions and relapse into sin."[38]

Even with the availability of confession, negative parenting that motivates with fear often results in Catholics presuming themselves bad. This apprehension frequently leads to begging and pleading not to be condemned or abandoned, but to be saved and restored to God's all-good parental love. This may account for the remarkably frequent requests for mercy found throughout liturgical prayers. "Lord Have Mercy" begins the Mass, "Lamb of God . . . have mercy on us" prepares the faithful for the Eucharist, while the priest silently utters "never let me be parted from you" and may the sacrament "not bring me condemnation, but health in mind and body."[39] Members of Fundamentalist religions, on the other hand, view salvation as "a single decisive event," wherein they choose Jesus Christ as their crucified Savior and risen Lord. By that one act they are born again and are given the gift of righteousness.[40] Should they backslide or fall again into worldly habits, they can repent of their ways and rededicate their lives to God.[41] There is no need for the continual pleading common with Catholics; Bible-based believers simply need to repent, cover themselves with the blood of Christ, and assume they are forgiven. In order to be given glory, honor, and peace, however, they persist in doing good for, should they choose a godless way of life, they will have a destiny filled with wrath and anger (Romans 2:6-11).[42]

GUILT

Conditional parents often raise guilt-ridden offspring. Healthy guilt is indicative of a well-developed conscience and helps individuals form right relationships with each other and act in accordance with their values. Conditional parents instill an unhealthy form of guilt by setting standards that are as unattainable as they are rigid. These measures of behavior are usually beyond human reach and allow for no deviation or error. Children raised by perfectionistic parents are often anxious, fearful, and guilty because somehow they realize they can never measure up to their parents' expectations no matter how hard they try. They may sense a vast chasm between who they are and what they are asked to do or be. Thus, because they equate approval with love, they never feel loved for themselves but only for the false self they present to the world.

The standards set by righteous religion are often cast in absolutes and allow for little deviation or shades of meaning. These regulations tolerate minimal disagreement or range of interpretation. Often members are led to believe that parental religion's standards are God's standards and that any difference of opinion or opposition to church laws is an indication of their irresponsibility and imperfection and not a flaw in the regulations themselves.

Leaders of authoritarian religion frequently cite numerous quotes from the Bible to keep believers in line. Should they fail to measure up to the standards set by their parental churches, such wayward children are often then regulated by guilt. Paul's passage to the Romans is used to remind the faithful of their former slavery to sin and the assumption that they should still be ashamed for their past behavior (Romans 6:20-21).[43] Further, members are told that any time they fall away after having tasted the heavenly gift, "they are crucifying the Son of God all over again and subjecting him to public disgrace" (Hebrews 6:4-6).[44]

Christ's admonition to his followers to be perfect even as his heavenly father is perfect (Matthew 5:28)[45] is sometimes called forth to persuade the faithful to live up to impossible standards. This striving for exceeding the human condition and attempting Christ-like excellence is reiterated in 2 Corinthians (13:9-11) where Paul prays for his follower to aim for perfection.[46] Thus, when Biblical quotes of a blaming or perfectionistic nature are presented to people, they often feel a sense of guilt when their response is less than perfect.

The *Baltimore Catechism*, a manual instrumental in the conscience formation of many adult Catholics, frequently sets a guilt-inducing tone, filled as it is with absolutes and dichotomies. For example, Catholics are admonished not to "waste their sufferings," lest they be sent to God's hospital for souls, Purgatory, where they must be cured by fire before entering Heaven.

> Only those who love God perfectly can enter heaven. But even many good people die with only a weak love of God. They had more interest in the people and the things of this earth than they did in God. They did not love Him with their whole heart and soul. They wasted many opportunities to please Him.[47]

The theme of loving God "enough" is also stressed by Bible-based religions which cite Christ's great commandment to love the Lord God with all ones heart, soul, strength and mind (Luke 10:27).[48] Unfortunately, guilt often results when preachers combine this wonderful ideal with the notion of being spit out of God's mouth when failing to give witness to it (Revelation 3:14-16).[49] People "witness" by accepting Jesus as a personal savior; by believing that the Bible is inspired, inerrant, and infallible; by making the personal decision to be baptized by immersion; by practicing daily devotions; and by sharing the good news of Jesus Christ. Anything that smacks of being lukewarm demonstrates an insufficient love of the Lord and indicates a less than full commitment to serving God.[50]

The church's emphasis on the perfect nature of God's parental love contrasted with imperfect, feeble human love is a constant source of guilt and shame for many believers. Not only must they struggle to be perfect, but righteous religion increases the pressure by elevating that struggle to a battle. In this regard Catholics are told: "A Catholic who never tries to work for the conversion of non-Catholics or to bring bad Catholics back to the sacraments is a soldier who lets the enemy win without putting up a fight."[51] The battle is not just with other human beings, but with an "infernal enemy" who is ". . . formidable, his courage undaunted, his hatred cruel and implacable, and his fury unmitigated. He wages against us a perpetual war. There can be on our part no peace with him and no cessation of hostilities."[52] Fundamentalists are warned to fight this enemy by donning the full armor of God, girding their loins in truth, putting on the breastplate of salvation, strapping on their "gospel shoes," taking up the shield of faith, assuming the helmet of salvation, and picking up the sword of the Spirit.[53]

By being responsible for matching God's perfect love, vigorously proselytizing for the faith, and conducting successful warfare with the devil, believers in authoritarian or righteous religion are set up for a rude awakening. Due to the sheer enormity of the tasks, there is little way that mere mortals can help but experience disappointment and disapproval from the parental church. With tasks so great, guilt so intense, spiritual self-esteem so low, it is no wonder that many Christians feel disillusioned by the very religions which have promised to stand by them through the traumas of life.

UNWORTHINESS AND SHAME

Shame is often a constitutive element in unworthiness and low self-esteem. Good parents seldom use shame as a method to control their children's behavior, but rather, provide instruction and guidelines while preserving the offspring's sense of self-worth. For example, when children feel humiliated or deeply embarrassed, "good enough" parents empathize with the feelings and then help them use the situation as a learning experience. In contrast, conditional parents capitalize on the shame and the accompanying sense of unworthiness, employing them as a means to control future misbehavior. Such parents may communicate either verbally or nonverbally that their children are stupid, worthless, clumsy, or bad, thus leaving offspring with an internalized sense of being defective and flawed at their very core.

Righteous religion functions in much the same way as a conditional parent. It can undermine self-esteem by frequent references to human unworthiness. This accentuates what is sometimes called the good/bad split wherein people shoulder badness and shame in order for God, parents, and even their churches to remain perfect and good. In this regard, *The Roman Catechism* teaches that "human beings are like spoiled children" with a weak and "corrupted nature." In their "fallen condition," if left to their own devices, they become "dupes of their own imprudence," amusing themselves with "frivolous conversations" and frittering away their time in "unprofitable pursuits." Further, without the help of religious authority "we rush onward toward our own voluntary destruction."[54]

Believers are inculcated with a sense of shame and are conditioned to believe that even their very faith can be defective. Much of the teaching provided by authoritarian religions inadvertently convinces members that they are morally and spiritually deficient and have inherited a condition of sinfulness. These churches convince members that at their very core they are slaves to sin, perverse, self-aggrandizing, anti-God, rebellious, weak, fallen, and possessed of a twisted heart,[55] in spite of the fact that, at the time of their conversion, they supposedly received a new heart and were cleansed by the blood of Christ.

Tracing humanity's inherent evil back to Adam and Eve (Genesis 3), preachers and church leaders have striven for ever new and fresh ways to impress upon the faithful their inherited legacy of pollution and shamefulness. In Romans, Paul is enlisted for his particularly pointed words assailing the human condition. People (supposedly non-believers) are characterized as godless fools, possessed of darkened hearts and gripped by sinful desires and shameful lusts. Further, they are "filled with every kind of wickedness, evil, greed, and depravity. They are full of envy, murder, strife, deceit and malice. They are gossips, slanderers, God-haters, insolent, arrogant, and boastful; they invent ways of doing evil; they disobey their parents; they are senseless, faithless, heartless, ruthless" (Romans 1:18-31).[56]

Those who are born again are told that these characteristics do not apply to them. Yet, after hearing descriptions of this nature on a regular basis, individuals might have a difficult time not internalizing them.

Themes of shame and unworthiness are threaded through many prayers of authoritarian religion. During the Mass, directly before the reception of Communion, Catholics recite, "Lord, I am not worthy to receive you."[57] In prayers seeking the Holy Mother's intercession, the faithful come to her "sinful and sorrowful," "mourning and weeping in this valley of tears," and ask her to "pray for us sinners now and at the hour of our death."[58] Shame is also inculcated into children at Fundamentalist churches who are taught to memorize the Sinners Prayer in order to someday become true Christians: "Dear Jesus. I know I am a sinner. Please forgive my sins. Thank you for dying on the cross for me. Come into my heart. Amen."[59]

Additionally, members of such churches are admonished once again to put on the *full* armor of God, since it does little good to put on only part of the necessary protection. Why? "Satan has an uncanny ability to play upon your weaknesses. If you are unprotected in a particular area, the devil will attempt to exploit that weakness."[60] Such language illustrates a foundational belief of authoritarian religion that sinfulness marks everyone from birth and that there is "a universal deformity to human nature."[61] Thus by stressing the corruption of the moral and spiritual nature of believers, in spite of having been saved, righteous religion capitalizes on the shame and unworthiness of its members to control their behavior.

CONTAINING EMOTIONS

"Good enough" parents believe that children's feelings are important and tolerate a reasonably wide range of emotional reactions. Such parents can see value in intense emotion, sometimes interpreting it as a passionate involvement in life. While they may validate emotional expressions as authentic, they help their children to channel them in appropriate and nondestructive ways. Conditional parents, on the other hand, frequently expect their offspring to deny and censor their feelings in order to maintain parental illusions about their own parenting, the nature of the children they have reared, or about the family in general. In such families, certain emotions are proscribed and others are countenanced.

Righteous religion can act like a conditional and potentially alienating parent when it disallows certain feelings and blesses others. For example, Christians are charged to abhor presumption, jealousy, lust and lustful thoughts, fear, bitterness, pride, arrogance, unbelief, resentment, anger, hatred, lukewarmness, indifference, ingratitude, despair, envy, homosexual temptations, and desires contrary to chastity.[62] The ever-reliable Paul offers his own list of emotions to be avoided: rage, anger, bitterness, every form of malice, any kind of impurity, and greed (Ephesians 4:31; 5:4).[63] On the other hand, the born again are to feel tranquil, patient, loving, generous, peaceful, affable, gentle, and forgiving.[64] Frequently quoted are scripture passages exhorting true believers to be kind, compassionate, holy, alert, self-controlled; to lead quiet lives while minding their own business; and to be joyful always, pray continually, and give thanks in all circumstances (Ephesians 4:32; 1 Thessalonians 4:11, 5:6,16-18).[65]

Even though believers are often told that they cannot lose their salvation, they are to keep their emotions bridled lest they fall prey to the devil. Members of righteous religion are warned that Satan works overtime attacking lax Christians with "evil thoughts, vile imaginations, and impure daydreams," eventually leading them to fear, doubt, and presumably perdition.[66] The demons of evil give humans a "proneness to sensual lusts and sinful pleasures," which results in individuals having to "battle for purity" and "to struggle against concupiscence of the flesh and disordered desires."[67] These cravings of sensuality fight against spiritual ideals and engage in assaults so numerous and attacks so varied "that it is extremely difficult to escape unhurt."[68]

Thus, members of authoritarian religion struggle continually against their "fallen nature." They must even guard against verbalizing their emotions, because their "mouth can either be a means of blessing and encouragement or cursing and death."[69] They are to keep a watch over the door of their lips (Psalms 141:3) so that they do not indulge in unwholesome or foolish talk (Ephesians 4:29; 5:4) or minced oaths such as "Judas priest," "Gosh," "Darn," or "Heck."[70]

Good parents help children pay attention to their bodies and be alert to how they are feeling. For such parents, the body is perceived as a valued and respected friend rather than as an abode of the enemy, which according to the Catholic church is not even to be wept over once the soul has departed.[71] Parental authoritarian religions ask the "frozen chosen" to maintain an "eternal smile" and never express their feelings unless they are positive.[72] Good Christians are to wage war upon their feelings, eradicate the poison of sinful emotions, and learn to control their bodies in a way that is holy and honorable (1 Thessalonians 4:4).[73]

CREATION OF DEPENDENCY

One of the goals of good parenting is to help children become self-reliant and take care of themselves in the world. "Good enough" parents strive to empower their offspring in such a way that they can think for themselves, make decisions, decide right from wrong, trust their own judgment, express disagreement, and take a stand. Conditional parents, on the other hand, rarely encourage initiative in their sons and daughters, fostering instead a sense of passivity, submissiveness, and docility. By being the sole and indisputable authority, they discourage their children from thinking and deciding for themselves and from becoming confident, self-reliant, assertive, and independent. Conditional parents rarely share power with the younger generation, but rather insist that offspring relinquish control of their lives and forever remain as children. Paradoxically, this overparenting, like underparenting, often leads to feelings of insecurity in children because both are equally devaluing of the personhood of the younger generation. Offspring from both types of family situations feel adrift, conflicted, and fragmented, lacking trust in themselves and their own resources. They frequently question their own maturity, judgment, competence, and often their very worth as beings.

Righteous religion assumes the role of conditional parent by positioning itself as the irrefutable authority in faith and morals over a faithful people who are to adhere loyally and obediently to its teaching.[74] As we have seen, such churches contend that they participate in God-ordained authority and any rebellion against that authority is a serious sin.[75] Authoritarian religions take the Bible as their starting point wherein "God purposes to direct the belief and behavior of his people through the revealed truth set forth in Holy Scriptures."[76]

Catholics believe that Scripture alone, without proper interpretation, is insufficient. Claiming for itself the role of "sole authentic interpreter of the Word of God," the Catholic church contends that its teaching or magisterium preserves in their entirety the things that God has revealed throughout the ages.[77] In this regard, the magisterium "must protect God's people from the danger of deviations and confusion, guaranteeing them the objective possibility of professing the authentic faith free from error, at all times and in diverse situations."[78] Thus, the church as a conditional parent not only knows best, but it apparently knows all. All Catholics are expected to recognize "the right of the pope, bishops, pastors, and priests to teach on behalf of the Lord Jesus."[79] These officials are mandated to act as teachers and rulers to lead God's people to the source of truth and holiness.[80] The pope, in particular, teaches Christ's revelation and "speaks with the bishops as the voice of Jesus Christ alive in the church."[81] Bishops, for their part, "have a sacred right and a duty before the Lord of legislating for and of passing judgment on their subjects."[82] They "are to be revered by all as witnesses of divine and Catholic truth," preaching the faith which informs the thinking and directs the conduct of the people assigned to them.[83]

Fundamentalist religion, on the other hand, finds God's truth in the teaching of Scriptures. Followers believe these writings are inspired, inerrant, sufficient, and clear.[84] In other words, Scripture is "God-breathed and is useful for teaching, rebuking, correcting and training in righteousness" (2 Timothy 3:16).[85] These churches maintain that scripture tells members all they need to know for salvation and eternal life and that it is "straightforward and self-interpreting on all matters of importance."[86] Further, for individuals who read scripture daily, meditate upon it, and commit it to memory, the Bible serves as the source of wisdom and is the final authority on all matters temporal and eternal. Thus, it is not unusual to see such believers sporting bumper stickers that state:

God said it.
I believe it.
That settles it.[87]

Like a conditional parent, authoritarian religion insists upon respectful obedience from the members. Catholics who truly desire eternal salvation within the church, "must cling to her and embrace her, like those who entered the ark to escape perishing." In fact, the church contends that "she is prefigured by Noah's Ark, which alone saves from the flood."[88] Rather than encouraging adult Catholics to think for themselves, the church calls for a loyal submission of will and intellect to all that it teaches regarding faith and morals.[89] Even if the faithful have an abiding and honest disagreement with the parental church, they are nonetheless to adhere unquestioningly to decisions made by the Holy Father, aligning themselves with the pope's "manifest mind and intention."[90] Should Catholics obstinately deny or doubt "some truth which must be believed with divine and Catholic faith," they are guilty of heresy.[91]

While Bible-based churches demand that the faithful submit all human thoughts to Scripture, this usually means giving obedience to God-ordained authority on earth. Referring to 1 Samuel, they state that rebellion is like divination (use of the occult to perceive the unknown) and that "to obey is better than sacrifice, and to heed is better than the fat of rams" (1 Samuel 15:22-23).[92] Righteous religions believe that they constitute "God's household, which is the church of the living God, the pillar and foundation of the truth" (1 Timothy 3:15).[93] In these churches, the deacon (or pastor, elder, or preacher) is to oversee and manage the children and household well. The faithful owe respect to these leaders who are over them and who bear the duty of admonishing them (1 Thessalonians 5:12).[94] Rebelling against this God-given authority is seen as a serious sin, almost like practicing witchcraft. "If spiritual rebellion is tantamount to divination, clearly this sort of rebellion is more than merely being an opinionated, strong-willed, or independent person. It is an attitude that sets itself up against God and his appointed representatives."[95]

SUMMARY

Righteous religion practices a form of parenting that is often conditional and thus detrimental to the spiritual maturity of the faithful. By means of frequent allusions to judgment and a questionable salvation, considerable anxiety is generated in believers over their possible exclusion by the parental church or the parental God. They know that failure to observe the rules can lead to unrighteousness or even damnation.

An essential ingredient of Fundamentalism's or authoritarian Catholicism's approach to parenting is the instillation of fear. Frequent catechetical or scriptural references to sin, the devil, and hell are held over the heads of the possible nonbelievers as a constant threat of everlasting separation from the parental God. Fear compels people to consider themselves as debased, depraved, flawed, and in constant need of repentance, in order to assure eternal salvation and acceptance. By exploiting fear, guilt, unworthiness, and shame, the conditional parenting of authoritarian religions reinforces the notion that the church is good and that the childlike believer is bad.

Members often feel guilty about not having met the expectations of God and their religion. Those who equate approval with love may sense themselves to be on the verge of banishment if they have displeased the church or its parental leaders. They can feel unworthy and ashamed, as if they are no longer God's children. Spontaneous, natural, and perhaps even healthy displays of emotion are curtailed for fear of incurring parental censure and possible estrangement. Thus, by staying in conformity with their authoritarian religion, believers may be losing the voices of their souls. In other words, to ensure that they remain in parental favor, they surrender the voice of their true selves. Given the conditional parenting of the church, some members have come to distrust their ability to make decisions. By devaluing their internal resources and wisdom, they have become alienated from their God-breathed intuition and the voice of the Spirit within.

Chapter 5

Clergy as Healthy Parents

Clerical leaders are not merely peripheral players in righteous religion, but rather, these individuals are the "power and focus of the cultural and religious meaning."[1] In other words, the clergy (who are almost always male in these churches)* are central participants in the drama of Christian life and are expected by many to be the embodiment of the abiding and loving (male) God. The priest, minister, or elder looms:

> As a key person–a particularly influential "Father"–in the formation of attitudes, self-images, and other elements of religious development. He is no less influential indirectly in the documents, institutional patterns, and even doctrines which he fashions and which in turn play their role in the religious development of persons.[2]

Generally speaking, members of authoritarian religions are conditioned to transfer onto clergy the same hopes, anticipations, and trust that they have invested in God or the church itself, in spite of the fact that Fundamentalists are told that Scripture alone is their only authority. Basically, however, Christians want priests or ministers to be parental and spiritual leaders who affirm their goodness, keep them safe and comforted, support their honest efforts to lead good lives, and provide spiritual guidance and nourishment. They desire the clergy to personify the image of the good shepherd, serving as overseers to the flock under their care (1 Peter 5:2),[3] leading them away from all that would do them harm.

---

*Because of this, masculine pronouns will be used when referring to clergy in authoritarian religions.

In their dealings with religious leaders, the faithful look for Christ-like individuals who exemplify a sense of justice, stability, fidelity, fairness, a well-ordered personal life, and a wholehearted commitment to the gospel. As such, the clergy are expected to be a people set apart from others. Their motivations are to be more noble, their vocations more sacred, their thoughts more pure, their lives more dedicated, and their sacrifices more generous.[4]

EMOTIONAL MAKEUP

Many would agree that these expectations are far too inflated for even the most saintly of human beings, and more often than not, they are beyond the capacities of most religious leaders. Given what studies have shown over the years about the psychological characteristics of religious professionals, clergy fall considerably short of their flock's vaunted expectations. Although much of the research on clergy, for reasons unknown, is rather dated, the older studies that are available describe the clergy by whom most middle-aged and older believers have been shepherded. Recent research, however, does confirm and validate these earlier findings, and points to a clerical profile that has changed little in over thirty years.

Instability

As much as believers would wish their religious leaders to be paragons of reliability and emotional solidity, studies have shown that generally this is not the case. Bible-based clergy suffer from the same mental problems (and to the same degree) as do members of their congregations. Thus, the number of clergy who are depressed, overly nervous, compulsive, and who otherwise experience emotional distress corresponds proportionately with the number of folks in the pews who suffer similar conditions.[5]

Catholic priests, on the other hand, compared to their congregations, have consistently demonstrated a higher degree of psychopathology and psychological dysfunctions.[6] Similarly, as a group, they possess a lower level of mental health, emotional functioning, and total adjustment than average Americans. For example, in the

National Conference of Catholic Bishops' 1985 report on "The Health of American Catholic Priests," of the 4,600 priests studied, 39.6 percent reported "severe personal, behavioral or mental problems" in the previous twelve months.[7] In the only extensive psychological study of the American priesthood ever conducted, 77 percent of the priests were described as either maldeveloped or underdeveloped.[8] The study "suggests a failure of growth on the part of priests rather than the presence of illness" and points to "capacities which have not been realized rather that the presence of psychological obstacles which can never be overcome."[9]

Identity

Candidates have often assumed an adult role most of their lives and continue to choose the clerical state as a way to continue to achieve adult or parental approval. Many such individuals make no conscious choice for the priesthood or ministry based on their own interests and abilities, but rather accede to the wishes and expectations of families and church communities. For them, "the clergy role appears a natural continuation of the little-adult role to which he has become accustomed, in which he has become proficient, and in which he has found important gratifications."[10]

Thus, it is not uncommon for the clergy to be blocked in the formation of their own identity and to "frequently assume the identity conferred upon them by others or through a role which they are asked to live, such as that of being a clergyman."[11] The notion of conforming to a role designated by others is attractive to the little adult. He has met the expectations of others all of his life. Likewise, he has trained himself to be good, to do well, and to know all the right answers.

The difficulty with little adults aspiring to the priesthood or ministry is that their role becomes a total definition of themselves and their attempt to be all things to all people can leave them "without a sense of identity at all."[12] This identity dilemma can be seen in Protestant seminarians who have been shown to have little insight into their own personalities, and in Catholic priests, the majority of whom are out of touch with their emotions and devote much energy trying to develop an idealized self (rather than a true self). In fact, three out of four priests have an incomplete idea of themselves, and thus have difficulty maintaining a stable or consistent personality.[13]

The picture presented by clergy operating under the parental approval of authoritarian religions, then, is one of individuals attempting to conform and mold themselves to the expectations of others. Thus, they are neither connected to their own voices of truth, nor fully alive to the Spirit breathing within them.

Inadequacy

Personal feelings of inadequacy echo like a strong underlying chord in the psyche of many clergy in authoritarian religions. The magical and "miracle making" roles often identified with the ministry are a natural draw for individuals who are striving to overcome personal inadequacies or to compensate for inferiority.[14] "Many psychological investigators have suggested that the pulpit is especially attractive to men who have strong inner conflicts to resolve."[15]

The clerical leadership of Fundamentalism and authoritarian Catholicism often grew up in homes where their own fathers were generally aloof and avoidant. In these distant relationships, the young boys were afforded little opportunity for paternal love and mentoring. Thus, the choice of the ministry was an attempt to obtain some of the respect, acceptance, and attention of which they had been deprived of as children.[16] In this regard, the church congregation becomes a father surrogate and, from it, priests and ministers struggle to earn the affirmation and affection they so sorely missed during their upbringing. The ministry, therefore, offers candidates a singular opportunity to gain entry into their father's house and a chance to resolve their childhood feelings of inferiority.

The childhood of these little adults who eventually choose the clerical state has been characterized by an excessive obedience and caution "for fear of sacrificing parental goodwill."[17] As adults, they have frequently been described as passive, submissive, and conforming with a strong desire not to offend their congregation, superiors and, by internal extension, their fathers. Hand in glove with this passivity, and likewise flowing from unresolved feelings of inadequacy, is a deep dependency. Clergy are often dependent upon the goodwill of others for their self-esteem and feelings of vocational success.[18]

To compensate for these less-than-desirable feelings of passivity and dependency, clerical leaders of authoritarian religions often assume an "idealized self-image." This view of themselves is a picture of what they would like to be, the role they feel they ought to be playing. The image is thought to bridge the gap between what they are and what they would like to be. As long as they are able to keep that image intact, unsullied, and viable, they can feel superior and harmonious inside. In spite of the illusory nature of their existence, they are no longer inadequate and passive children in little adult bodies and roles. After all, "what could be less passive than to be in the pulpit, called by God to change the world?"[19]

Superiority

Individuals who are drawn toward ministry in righteous authoritarian religions are most often those who are compensating for low self-esteem. As mentioned previously, many were reared in homes where they felt uncertain about their worth and lovability. Thus, such individuals gravitated toward the clerical state wherein they could enjoy the prestige and importance that automatically come with the role of minister or priest.

The attraction to righteous religion can be traced to the parenting experienced by many future clergy. In childhood they frequently lived in homes where "family government was authoritarian and rigorously repressive. Parental authority was absolute, and exercised without checks or control by anyone else in the household. Obedience and submission were the only acceptable responses for children."[20] Parents in such households were concerned with control and maintaining order. Coercion was perfectly acceptable and obedience was often obtained by force rather than by consent, example, or persuasion. Children in authoritarian homes were raised in an atmosphere where "absolute and unquestioning obedience to authority" was expected and youngsters were subjected to a great deal of fear and intimidation. "The polarities of order and disorder, obedience and rebelliousness"[21] are the enduring legacies of these homes. Children, even infants, were seen as depraved and potentially damned and the parents felt deeply responsible for putting the fear of the

Lord in little ones lest they succumb to their perverse wills. Knowing that the chasm between salvation and eternal banishment was immeasurable, parents felt justified in doing everything possible to ensure subservience and compliance to the parental conscience.

Many members of the clergy replicate in their ministerial work the patterns of their childhood. Their zealously religious parents were often engaged in a war with their offspring, "a war which could end only with total victory by the parents and unconditional surrender by the child."[22] These clergy, then, bring into their ministry concepts such as fear of God, obedience, control, depravity, damnation, and warfare. Thus, it is not surprising that these themes seem to thread themselves through the practices of authoritarian righteous religion.

Often authoritarian ministers and priests continue their childhood warfare with their own congregations. In a sense, then, they have become like their own parents, battling the demons within the children who are under their care. Comparatively speaking, clergy operating in domineering religions are more authoritarian than their mainstream counterparts, manifest a greater need to control, tend toward self-sufficiency and dominance, and are more likely to impose obedience upon the faithful.[23]

Given that their role requires them to be bearers of truth, guardians of souls, shapers of conscience, and proclaimers of sacred teachings, clergy in righteous religions often tend to compensate for lifelong feelings of inadequacy by denying any weakness.[24] To undertake their lofty, reverential role, they assume the modeling of their parents, projecting an air of superiority, dominance, and a high sense of personal worth. Given that many believe that the salvation of their congregation rests with them, they adopt the certainty and closed-mindedness so characteristic of the morally righteous.[25]

Catholic priests may have an additional motivation for projecting a sense of superiority. Like classic company men, they desire the status and power that comes with promotion within the Catholic hierarchical system. In fact, those who appear the most successful or well adjusted among the Catholic clergy are often those who are most intent on law, order, power, and the exercise of authority. Their lives are characterized by a tone of self-righteousness, "one that disposes them to seek power and authority because they look on themselves as the rightful inheritors of these."[26]

Isolation

The ministry by its very nature often produces within its practitioners a sense of isolation. Most church members have a tendency to set their religious leaders apart, perhaps in the belief (or hope) that these individuals are monolithic "Rocks-of-Gibraltar," requiring time for study, prayer, or contemplation.[27] Isolation is further intensified by congregations when they overly scrutinize these idealized and pedestal-dwelling leaders, possibly in an effort to ensure that they live up to the expectations they are supposed to embody.

This fishbowl-like, set-apart lifestyle is often very alluring to individuals who had lonely childhoods since, for them, the ministry replicates their original home or environment. Many who feel called to a career in religion, in fact, may be attracted to a "refuge vocation," where "set-apartness and emotional distance" are inherent in the role.[28] Clergy are able to "play it safely aloof," thus providing a harbor for the introversion that disposed them to religious life in the first place.[29] Introverted individuals are usually introspective and some, due to their tendency to focus inward, lack interpersonal skills. Research findings suggest that the picture of a typical clergy member includes introversion, distance from others, and a lack of confidence regarding personal relationships.[30] Some studies occasionally describe the clergy as extroverted rather than introverted.[31] In these cases, the "little adult" is undoubtedly at work, convincingly acting out the role of ingratiating host, paterfamilia, and beloved pastor. Conservative Protestant clergy have been found to be more socially introverted than their liberal counterparts and to possess fewer interpersonal skills. Furthermore, conservative religious leaders tend to experience difficulty in establishing warm and intimate relationships.[32]

Catholic clergymen closely resemble conservative Protestant ministers. Studies have shown that priests are often socially inept, withdrawn, introverted, shy, retiring, self-conscious, and ill-at-ease in forming relationships with others.[33] One author noted the "generalized lack of closeness with anybody in their lives . . . one is struck by the human isolation of these men, the almost unconnected manner in which they lead their lives, even though they find themselves in the midst of people all the time."[34] Further, the upcoming generation of Catholic priests appears to be as socially withdrawn and isolated as ordained priests. A study of 152 seminarians found that future leaders are also introverted, nonconforming, and uncomfortable with their ability to maintain interpersonal relationships. As a group, these seminarians experience anxiety over their lack of emotional fulfillment due to a need for affection and interpersonal relationships.[35]

Hostility

The pulpit often acts as an ineluctable magnet for those who need an outlet for their feelings of conflict and hostility. Below the righteous and virtuous facade worn by many leaders of authoritarian religion, there exist "deep-seated feelings of hostility and rebellion."[36] Data suggest that students for the ministry, when compared with students from the disciplines, display more discomfort with hostile feelings and are more self-punishing in handling aggressive feelings. Further, some research points to the inability of Catholic priests "to cope with aggressive feelings and a lack of sensitivity to respond to their own needs and feelings."[37] Thus, unresolved childhood rage and a desire to strike back at offending authority figures fuels the behavior of many authoritarian ministers and priests.

The genesis of this rage may be found in the harsh manner with which the Bible was interpreted and implemented in the homes of many prospective religious leaders. "So much Christian theology has been rooted in the threat of punishment that we need to be aware of the personal experiences that have made such theologies sensible and powerfully appealing to so many people for such a long time."[38] The previously discussed home atmosphere of control and obedience frequently included biblically sanctioned corporal punishment such that authoritarian religions are among the most outspoken defenders of physical punishment. Themes of discipline, suffering, control, chastising, and not sparing the rod have been theologically sanctioned by twenty centuries of organized Christianity. The proverbs of the Old Testament have been quoted to justify "two thousand years of physical violence and painful assaults against the bodies, spirits, and wills of children."[39] Martin Luther, who was beaten and whipped as a child, is typical of many clergy insofar as he incorporated his childhood wounds into his theology and ministry. The consequences of his punishments resonated "through the lives of countless Puritans, evangelicals, and fundamentalists in the New World as well as in Europe."[40] Thus, for Luther, his historical counterparts and subsequent generations of authoritarian clergy, the enduring rages originating in childhood smolder within and reverberate through their congregations.

The clerical state offers candidates a lifestyle in which wrath and fury can be channeled and kept under moral control. In other words, aggression is redirected toward the greater glory of God, the church, or scriptural ideals.[41] Anger becomes righteous and legitimate when focused upon the forces of Satan and the sin inherent in moral issues such as homosexuality, abortion, secular humanism, and feminism. When engaging in "spiritual warfare," authoritarian clergy can give full throttle to their hostility since they are "warriors for Christ." Satan is the enemy and anger at the Evil One is praiseworthy. The rage bottled up from childhood is thus given a target and preachers can encourage others to become "mad enough to stand up and fight back in the power of Jesus' name."[42]

Since clergy are often quite uncomfortable or ambivalent about their conflicting or aggressive feelings, they may repress them, covering them over with a facade of submissiveness, passivity, and soft-spokeness. Ministers and priests who feel an incongruence between their inner rage and the image of the loving savior are often at war with themselves. To reconcile this discrepancy, they enact their Christ-like self-image, behaving in every way possible like the good shepherd. By assuming this role, they must exclude from awareness the hostility present since childhood. Thus, most of the time the faithful see only the gentle Jesus in their pastors. Sometimes, however, the people will see the deep-seated anger flaring out, or be disturbed by the incongruous spectacle of this peace-loving, reconciling Christ-figure advocating intolerance and spiritual warfare.

Sexual Conflicts

While Christianity has a history of repressing the sensual and sexual (the acceptance of marriage for the Protestant clergy notwithstanding), practitioners of authoritarian forms of Christianity are especially zealous in stressing the split between body and soul. Unrelenting emphasis has been placed on purity, chastity, the shameful nature of sexual sins, as well as the suppression of sensual desires, lust, and carnal impulses. Even when acted upon in the theologically sanctioned state of matrimony, sex is often associated with guilt and shame. Within the Christian imagination, the words most often related to human sexual desire have included impure, unclean, abomination, immodest, filthy, vile, perverse, and sinful.

Little wonder, then, that studies of clergy point to large areas of psychosexual conflict, unavowed sexuality, discomfort with sexual feelings, and, not surprisingly, guilt.[43] Here again, there is evidence of the split in ministerial expectations between becoming like the gentle Jesus on the one hand and being a warrior for the Kingdom on the other. The clergy are called to an ambivalent state where the mandate to be a self-assertive, manly soldier of Christ conflicts with the Christian ideal to be "self-denying, will-less, subject and submissive, humble and meek, chaste and pure–all supposedly female attributes."[44] This inherent dilemma makes many in the clergy question their own masculinity, leaving them in a quandary about how to be a man in the ministerial role.

Combine this gender identity predicament with the background of sexual repression within which they were raised and the result is often individuals who are contending with "inner conflicts over sexuality and sexual identity."[45] For many attracted to the clerical state there is a "persistent theme of guilt" intimately related to struggles over the nature of their sexuality. By setting themselves apart in the ministry, many in the clergy are able "to reconcile some of the conflicting elements at war within the self."[46]

A large number of clergy in authoritarian religions have not achieved an integrated psychosexual identity. With negative or non-existent education concerning sexual development, many have experienced few of the trials and errors related to the budding sexuality of adolescence. Lacking the sufficient building blocks of sexual formation, many ministers and priests find that their sexual feelings are a great source of conflict and experience difficulty in blending sexuality smoothly and harmoniously into their lives.

For Catholic priests in particular, a great deal of effect is devoted to adjusting to celibacy. The strong psychological controls used by most of them "drain away an inordinate amount of energy and time in these priest's lives," which produces not the intended freedom for the kingdom of God, but rather intense anguish, concern, and uneasiness. Sexuality, then, is not integrated in the lives of many priests, which leaves them "functioning at a pre-adolescent or adolescent level of psychosexual growth."[47]

Moral Development

Not only is the sexual growth of many in the clergy arrested at an early stage, but so also are other areas of development. Priests and ministers in righteous authoritarian religions can be best understood if it is acknowledged that they often show "less Christian maturity than other [church] workers" and "that they have not accomplished the tasks which are appropriate to the developmental period known as adolescence."[48] It is during this stage that individuals form a reliable and consistent sense of their own personalities and learn to be themselves in close relationships with other people. True adults, as compared with adolescents, have stable personalities and can brave the sorrows and hazards involved in forming significant relationships without losing who they are. In other words, they can be themselves with others and chart a direction in life that is right for them. As has been already demonstrated in this chapter, many clergy in authoritarian religions have not accomplished these developmental tasks. The churches created by these individuals for whom growth has been blocked basically reflect the same level of underdevelopment as the majority of their clergy. According to psychiatrist Marianne Benkert Sipe, "it is clear that the institutional church is in a preadolescent stage of male psychosexual development."[49] In the period described by Dr. Sipe, typically prior to eleven years of age, girls are held in disdain by boys who play games of power and competition. Sex role socialization is intense and "sex generally is rigidly denied externally while secretly explored. The rigidity extends to strict rules of inclusion and exclusion. Control and avoidance are of primary concern."[50]

Authoritarian religions' emphasis on control, legalism, and strict standards of behavior and thought affects the moral and spiritual development of members. One of the most commonly acknowledged descriptions of moral development is the three-level theory of Lawrence Kohlberg.[51] On his first level are those whose motivations for doing the right thing center around the avoidance of punishment and serving their needs. People on the second level do what is right in order to look good and to maintain the established order and values of their community, be that family, neighborhood, or local church group. Level three individuals see beyond the perspectives of their own insular group and are committed to their own chosen, often evolving, ethical principles.

People's faith is expressed differently depending upon their level of moral development.[52] As moral reasoning and faith grow from level one to level three, there is a significant expansion in people's ways of thinking, ability to assume the perspectives of others different from themselves, imagery for the Divine, and tolerance for others' viewpoints. Whereas those on level one and two rely on fear and external authority as a basis for decision making and conscience formation, those on level three rely mainly on their own internal resources and overall sense of integrity.

Authoritarian religions both attract and are sustained by individuals on the first and second levels. In fact, "the self-centeredness of much of contemporary Christianity is representative of the . . . level one believer."[53] The faith of these people is shaped primarily by church authorities or by influences outside of themselves. Rules, laws, conventions, clear statements concerning right and wrong, punishments, and rewards are essential to guide moral decisions. People whose primary concerns center around their own personal salvation, rather than social justice or global issues, gravitate toward the certainty provided by righteous authoritarian religions. In these churches, personal moral decision making is largely limited to whether or not to follow the decrees of Scripture or church authority.

When studying members of authoritarian religions, most research has indicated a low level of moral reasoning. Level three, or principled moral reasoning, has seldom been found within Fundamentalist denominations.[54] Thus, it seems that neither heightened exposure to religious education, nor high levels of religions commitment, nor a large degree of religious orthodoxy results in morally mature individuals.[55] None of these efforts appear to produce highly developed people who exemplify what Scripture requires of them, namely "to act justly and to love mercy and to walk humbly with your God" (Micah 6:8).[56] Rather than mindful, freely chosen, and deeply reflective moral decision making, many believers in authoritarian religions are content to do what external authority mandates.

It is a moot question as to whether believers call forth the leadership they need, or whether leaders gather around themselves disciples reflective of their own moral depth. But when students for ministry in authoritarian religions were tested for moral judgment, they were found to be comparable to ninth graders. The minds of these seminarians "checked out" when confronted with items that required reasoned considerations of justice or a depth of reflection about moral principles. They simply sidestepped such items in favor of questions where scriptural tenets could more easily be applied. "Some even refused to rate items which they could not infuse with religious meaning."[57]

Many Catholic priests exhibit no more religious maturity than these Protestant seminarians. A major study of priests showed that they frequently demonstrated a "general inability to articulate a deep level of personal religious faith."[58] A majority had not developed a sustaining spirituality or philosophy of life and their faith seemed to reflect their lack of depth as persons. For those clergy, the priesthood may "offer them a setting in which they can survive without growing."[59]

Authoritarian religions place high value on communicating the right content of their faith, on preserving the letter of the law, on interpreting scripture literally, and on avoiding heresy or, for Catholics, not violating the church's magisterium. By restricting attention to only the right answers and keeping people within the boundaries of certain mandates, authoritarian churches essentially close the minds of the faithful. This narrowing of focus shackles members to legalism, and restricted definitions of right behavior. In these systems, believers feel a pressure to keep themselves safe from anything that might trouble them or make them question scripture, tradition, and the interpretations of their leaders. By neither allowing nor encouraging their members to probe their moral and religious questions, righteous religions effectively eliminate the ability to achieve a mature faith and the courage to speak with the voice of the Spirit that dwells within.[60]

ROLE OVERLOAD

Besides such internal factors as instability, inadequacy, superiority, isolation, hostility, sexual conflicts, and moral development, the external strains and impossible demands of the clerical role undermine priests' and ministers' ability to be the healthy parental figures so desired by the faithful. In this regard, most clergy spend about 50 percent of their time acting as organizers and administrators when in fact they are more comfortable undertaking the roles of pastor, preacher, priest, and teacher. Many who entered the ministry or priesthood hoping to exercise their true social and artistic talents find themselves intensely frustrated by being forced to act largely in the roles of enterprisers and managers.[61]

Ministers, as compared to Catholic priests, are asked to balance married life with an often self-perceived career of dedicated selfless service. But, how do spouses compete with Almighty God, and how do ministers manage the pressures to exemplify a marriage made in heaven? The role of pastor often clashes with the roles of husband and parent, leaving many in the ministry feeling overwhelmed and dispirited. Considering this, it should come as no surprise that among professional groups, the clergy ranked third in the number of divorces granted each year.[62]

Theologian H. Newton Malony believes that "seemingly professional ministry is a position that is hazardous to one's well-being."[63] Clergy burnout is common and 75 percent of them have experienced major stress in their work lives. Compared to the general population, ministers and priests exhibit "greater role overload, role ambiguity and role responsibility."[64]

In regard to the Catholic clergy, "priests' morale today seems particularly fragile."[65] Beset by diminishing numbers, greater work loads, and increasing expectations from both hierarchy and congregations, priests often feel caught in the middle and demoralized. Many feel trapped, overworked, and underaffirmed. Combine all this with the general underdevelopment of priests and what results is often a situation where some are promoted beyond their capabilities and are subjected to responsibilities that exceed their abilities to cope. The common experience of loneliness, a clouded personal future, and the sense that they have little or no control over their lives contribute to many priests feeling bone weary.[66]

Given the immensity of inner and outer pressures, it is little wonder that so many clerical and religious scandals occur. Clergy malpractice, whether involving sexual misconduct, child molestation, financial mismanagement, or improper counseling has become an emerging field of law. Ministers, who are expected by the faithful to exemplify ideal family relationships, are particularly vulnerable to sexual temptation. In one study, 13 percent of Protestant clergy surveyed reported that they had sexual intercourse with a church member other than their spouse–a number double that reported by members of other helping professions.[67]

Financial scandals likewise have proliferated, eroding the trust many have invested in authoritarian religions. In one instance, ministers in a Bible-based church were found guilty in federal court for conspiracy to commit fraud and money laundering in a $7 million investment scheme.[68] Jim Bakker was sent to prison for his financial misadventures. Scandals and rumors of financial misdeeds have rocked the Vatican bank and have been the subject of continuous media coverage.

To offset their losses, many churches feel compelled to obtain malpractice insurance. For example, Preferred Risk Mutual of Iowa insures some 26,000 churches and has paid out thousands of dollars in out-of-court settlements. Church Mutual of Wisconsin, which insures 15,000 churches in thirty states, has settled about a dozen claims. Catholic churches have been so impacted by financial burdens, precipitated in large part by clerical sexual misconduct, that insurance premiums are more than $200,000 per year, with annual deductibles of $500,000 and an annual limit of $1 million.[69]

The clerical role requires priests and ministers to be too many things to too many people. Combine this role overload with a system-imposed thwarting of a healthy psychosexual development, and what often results is sexual behavior considered inappropriate for members of the clergy. In other words, many in the clerical state have not been allowed to "try on" sexual exploration in adolescence and young adulthood and, thus, behave in ways that might be viewed as the equivalent of adolescent experimentation. Catholic priests, for example, are rarely helped in their seminary training to achieve an adult level of psychosexual integration. Being sexually "young" and underdeveloped, it is understandable yet lamentable that some choose children or adolescents as sexual partners. In fact, about twice as many Catholic priests (4 to 6 percent) as compared to Protestant clergy (2 to 3 percent) either act on a persistent attraction to children or display a sexual interest in youth. Another factor for this discrepancy between denominations is that Protestant ministers are more apt to be fired for sexual misconduct by the congregation that hired them, while the Catholic clergy, owing their allegiance directly to bishops, have been shielded and simply reassigned to other parishes.[70]

By imposing roles too heavy to shoulder in a system which allows little room for growth, maturity, and individuality, Fundamentalism and authoritarian Catholicism have created a situation which is demoralizing for both the clergy and believers. This demoralization is manifested by a growing lack of trust on the part of church members. They are beginning to vote their lack of confidence in church structures and leadership with their wallets and checkbooks. Where scandal has erupted in Bible-based churches, the faithful reacted with a drop in contributions (i.e., the Jim Bakker and Jimmy Swaggart scandals). The financial condition of the Catholic Church has been described as a "monetary disaster area." In the 1960s, Catholics contributed 2.2 percent of their income to their churches; thirty years later, that number was down to 1.1 percent, an estimated loss of $6 billion per year.[71]

CONCLUSION

Given the various issues and dynamics impacting the lives of ministers and priests, it is not surprising that many members of authoritarian religion are having second thoughts about their leadership. In fact, what people may be witnessing are clergy whose lack of personal growth, poorly realized religious faith, emotional defendedness, fragile morale, and sheer fatigue renders them incapable of assuming or implementing their parental roles. This clerical stultification shapes the tone and tenor of righteous religion and creates a condition of inconsistency and ambivalence for numerous adherents.

This situation of inconsistency and ambivalence hurts many thoughtful, maturing ministers and priests as well. Financial and sexual scandals, top-down authoritarian leadership, intolerance of dissent, anti-intellectualism, innuendoes, and lack of trust, all take their toll. "Loyal, hardworking, self-sacrificing men . . . watch helplessly as the reputation of a profession they love is torn to shreds and cast under chilling suspicion."[72] Some sadly and, after great struggle, leave. Although there are few studies describing the personalities of those who have resigned, one report indicates that Catholic priests who quit often cite the emotional cost of celibacy and loneliness as outweighing their sense of job satisfaction. Further, such leavers usually hold modern sets of values, are relatively young, and are inner-directed.[73] The clergymen who remain with a modicum of adjustment often do so at the expense of their personal growth and by keeping focused on the future, as well as by possessing a high regard for themselves and their work.[74] Such priests "substitute ambition and power for any real development of their personalities."[75] Given all that has been written in this chapter paralleling ministers with priests in authoritarian religions, it undoubtedly is quite safe to say that a significant number of Protestant clergy are departing (or remaining) for reasons similar to those of their Catholic counterparts. Thus, those who continue to serve are often little adults who cover up feelings of inadequacy and insecurity with an illusion of superiority and dogmatic righteousness.

This clerical underdevelopment has become institutionalized by a phenomenon known as projection. In this process, the structures of authoritarian religion actually become mirrors of the clergy, reflecting the same levels of dependency, compliance, restriction of emotions, and themes of shame and unworthiness. Much scriptural interpretation or moral theology is fraught with clerical/parental notions of evil lurking within themselves and, by extension, within everyone else. In view of their inner array of unexpressed anxieties, underdeveloped clergy keep church members as constricted as they are by projecting and systematizing their own need for rules and penalties concerning loyalty and compliance. In other words, to channel their own sense of insecurity and to curtail their own perfectionism, they assume that others need the same containment as they do. Hence, there is a tendency to overparent and overcontrol.

The clergy's lack of development shapes the major elements of their religion, particularly their image of God. People who are emotionally underdeveloped tend to focus their lives on legalism, dogmatism, and moralism and often feel shame, doubt, and fear when they don't live up to innumerable high standards. Accordingly then, God, for many priests and ministers, is the one who keeps score, requires placating, and is ready to punish for the least mistake. A judgmental God seems to resonate with authoritarian clergy's sense of incompleteness, "badness" (as in the good/bad split) and inferiority. As is typical of the projective process, clerics often assume that others see God in the same way. It is a short step, therefore, to concretizing this assumption and developing a religion which institutionalizes and theologizes the projections of the underdeveloped.

What may be happening is that believers are maturing and are outgrowing their clergy and the projective religious principles and practices constructed from their clergy's underdevelopment. In other words, while priests and ministers remain static in their development, numerous members are growing up, assuming their own voices, and struggling to become faithful to themselves and their ideals. Rather that requiring clear directives from outside themselves, they are realizing identities strong enough to embrace the tensions of ambivalence. As such, they are experiencing growing pains as they hear the Spirit speaking within them. Contrasted with the large number of clergy whose identity is defined by their roles, maturing Christians are relinquishing their roles as compliant and obedient children and are on the journey toward discovering their true voices.

PART TWO:
ONE BIG HAPPY FAMILY

Introduction

The twofold purpose of this section is to discuss: (1) how authoritarian righteous religions operate as family systems; and (2) how the process of conditional parenting and the clerical parents themselves function within those family systems to stifle the voices of maturing members. As has been demonstrated in previous chapters, Catholicism and Fundamentalism purport to be families, taking on familial terminology and roles. Further, the structure of these religions, their organization, and ways of operating seem to justify their being called systems. Theories involving systems incorporate the concept of wholeness whereby "a system cannot be understood by dissection and study of its individual parts."[1] Thus, to understand how a particular family operates, even a church family, it is important to look beyond the actions of individual members and observe how all family members operate and interact with one another. The perspective taken by family systems theory, then, is to focus on the entire family unit, asking not *why* something happened but *what* is going on in an effort to understand the patterns of interaction among and between members.[2]

The following section, then, will talk about righteous religions in terms of family systems and explore major interactional processes working within church environments. This discussion will provide insight into the workings of authoritarian religions and elucidate how these organizational systems provide a structure that is less than healthy for the clergy/parents, as well as potentially exclusionary, fear-producing, shame-based, emotionally alienating, and dependency-creating for members. It will be shown how, in their efforts to maintain cohesiveness and balance, righteous religions employ systems which impair spiritual and emotional maturity by offering little flexibility for change and development, stifling the voices of both the ordinary and the prophetic, and allowing little opportunity for open communication or negotiation of differences.

The topics in Part Two (Chapters 6 through 16) are arranged sequentially and build upon each other in introducing readers to systems theory. Ideally, both Catholic and Bible-based examples would be used to illustrate the concepts within each chapter, or at least Catholic and Fundamentalist illustrations would alternate with each chapter. Unfortunately, given the greater degree of hierarchical structure in Catholicism, some systems concepts better lend themselves to either Bible-based or Catholic examples. Thus, the sequencing of the following chapters may appear disproportionate with three Fundamentalist stories followed by three Catholic stories. Have faith, each chapter contains relevant insights for all readers.

Chapter 6

What Will People Think?

A righteous religion, much like a family, is an "emotional relationship system." According to Murray Bowen, people are emotionally enmeshed or intertwined in their families to varying degrees.[1] Some are totally entangled with the family, possessing little ability to think independently; others are connected to the family, yet still able to make their own choices.

Bowen's principle of enmeshment applies to the church in that being raised in authoritarian religions shapes self-definition, beliefs, values, and emotional reactions. All members are fused to their church to some extent but the degree of enmeshment varies, with most people finding themselves somewhere in the middle of a hypothetical scale. At one end of this "differentiation of self" scale[2] are those who can actively stay in relationship with the church yet remain self-determined. Some schools of thought call this position the "self-in-relation,"[3] wherein the bond or union is maintained, yet the selves or identities of the parties involved remain separate. Such members are able to express and act upon their own convictions whether or not these conform to official teaching or group pressure. At the other end of the continuum are those who have incorporated the ideals and standards of their religion to the extent that their very identities have been engulfed or absorbed by the mind of the parental church.[4] The story that follows illustrates how individuals with unformed and undifferentiated personalities who are emotionally fused with authoritarian religion can be extremely vulnerable when they find themselves in circumstances that run contrary to the moral dictates of their church family.

Paulette had loved Calvary Fellowship for as long as she could remember. It had taken on even greater importance since her husband had left her with two small children ten years ago. At age thirty-six, she found herself deeply involved in the organizations of her church, devoting time to teaching Sunday school, singing in the choir, and helping with the Missionary Society. The work Paulette did for Calvary Fellowship compensated for the acceptance and self-esteem she had lost when Marty left her for another woman. She was so desperate for validation that she frequently went overboard to win approval, being the first to volunteer for nearly every project. She was so anxious to please that other church members would become frustrated by her constant questions and comments reflecting uncertainty about herself: "Is it right to feel this way?" "Do you think the pastor would like this?" "I hope I'm doing the right thing."

For the past ten years, she had conducted herself as if she were still married in God's eyes and had declined the infrequent requests for dates. No one was more surprised than Paulette when she met Bart and was completely swept off her feet. Their first sexual encounter simply "happened" and resulted in her pregnancy. She was so frightened and confused that she consented to Bart's pressure to have an abortion. A counselor at the abortion clinic encouraged her to participate in a support group with other women in similar circumstances but Paulette could not bring herself to face them. The only time she ever mentioned the abortion was when she sought counsel with a visiting Evangelist whom she knew she would never see again.

Even repenting and rededicating her life to Jesus didn't succeed in soothing Paulette's conscience. She felt overwhelming waves of guilt about killing her own child, especially when the pastor and the Calvary Fellowship's Right to Life group referred to women like herself as murderers. She was terrified that she would be rejected by the congregation if the awful truth about herself were known and she vowed that they would never discover her secret. She needed approval and acceptance so desperately that she willingly conformed her thoughts and behavior to the expectations of her church community. She took care not to offend or disagree with anyone and many considered her the perfect Christian woman.

The conditional parenting of righteous religion seems to foster the ideal that Paulette embodies, that of a person completely dependent, selfless, unconditionally ready to serve, and willing to surrender her will to that of God-breathed authority at any given moment. While voluntarily surrendering one's will to God is a basic principle of spirituality, Paulette's fusion with parental religion is motivated less by a relationship with God and more by her fears of exclusion. Murray Bowen (as well as James Masterson who was discussed in earlier chapters) would describe Paulette's motivation as coming from the false or "pseudo-self" which is "designed to conform to the expectation of the immediate social group."[5] In contrast, "the person with the solid-self [or true self] operates on the basis of clearly defined beliefs, opinions, convictions and life principles developed through the process of intellectual reasoning and the consideration of alternatives."[6]

There is very little of Paulette that isn't heavily influenced by either the views of the church or the reactions of other people. She is constantly vulnerable to outside opinion and thus lives in a reactive rather than proactive manner, allowing the church community to make most of her decisions rather than deciding for herself. People such as Paulette "are totally relationship-oriented, devoting enormous amounts of energy to seeking love, approval, and validation."[7] Because of her intense needs for inclusion, combined with her terror of being separated from her religion, Paulette looks like the perfect Christian woman when actually her enmeshment with the church and low differentiation of self are hindering her from a mature, mindful spirituality.

Chapter 7

To Thine Own Self Be Untrue

LOYALTY

Authoritarian religion's spoken and unspoken demands for loyalty foster in many members an almost selfless enmeshment with this organizational family. Loyalty, in and of itself, however, is essential in families. It constitutes "the glue that holds families together, helps people make sacrifices for altruistic goals, and provides hope for the future."[1] As we have seen, loyalty is cultivated in the church similar to the way it is in families with the parental church serving as a protector, provider, nurturer, educator, and repository of family history. For its members, their religion has been present at times of birth, death, and trouble; has helped them celebrate the happy occasions of marriage and baptism; and may have provided a safe place to be with God. These experiences and services create in individuals a sense of indebtedness to the parental church. People feel this obligation to a greater or lesser extent. For some, the debt is small and the payments in self-determination and individuation are likewise small. For others, "the repayment cuts deeply into an individual's autonomy."[2]

Some Christians experience a continual need to meet their obligations of loyalty to their religion. It's as if an invisible "ledger"[3] keeps account of the repayment due to the church body not only for its aforementioned parental services, but also for providing the only sure way to guarantee eternal salvation. Thus, the compelling need to balance a largely unbalanceable ledger of indebtedness leaves these people feeling guilty and inescapably bound to authoritarian religion on many levels. The perceived need to maintain parental religion's approval and love by discharging their debts

83

deters many Christians from meeting obligations for their own maturity and growth. In other words, indebtedness to righteous religion may prevent members from ever feeling the pains and uncertainties of exclusion, but at the expense of personal individuation. Family systems theory refers to this condition of permanent ledger imbalance as "pathogenic relational configuration" wherein "the child is always in debt to the parent and becomes burdened by the guilt of undischarged obligations."[4]

In families such as the parental authoritarian church where balancing the ledger of indebtedness is a virtual impossibility, many members will not "become separate individuals in their own right" but rather remain dependent and enmeshed in the system. These kinds of families demand "loyalty in the form of absolute devotion" and frequently social development is sacrificed as proof of their loyalty and devotion.[5]

Tom and Marilyn, both aged forty-eight, were considered to be the "pillars" of the Jerusalem Bible Church. He was an elder and she was a leader of the youth group. When Christian Marriage Enrichment became popular, they were among the first to attend it and later were named regional officers of the organization. Their five children had attended Sunday School and publicly took Jesus as their personal Savior and Lord at one of the yearly revival meetings. It was on their twenty-eighth anniversary that Marilyn told Tom that she wanted a divorce. She could no longer tolerate his rigid, overbearing style of being what he referred to as "head of the household." He ran his family like a military unit and every decision, however small, required his approval. Tom had refused Marilyn's request to work outside the home, stating that her duty was to him and the scriptural mandate to obey her husband. This action was the last straw for Marilyn and, after a great deal of soul searching and inner turmoil, proved to be the impetus for the divorce.

Jerusalem Bible Church had been good to Marilyn over the years. Through it, she and her children found the salvation necessary to have their names written in the Book of Life. Further, the church helped celebrate her twenty-fifth wedding anniversary and her parent's fiftieth and had officiated at the deaths of her stillborn child and aged father. The congregation also had given her a sense of belonging and had rallied around her and her family at these times of joy and sorrow. Marilyn felt a deep loyalty to the church and an equally strong need to repay that indebtedness with a lifetime of faithful devotion and service. Because she owed so much to Jerusalem Bible Church and its teachings, she experienced enormous guilt over her resolution to divorce Tom. Not only would she hurt Tom and the children, but also she would irreparably impair her relationship with the church and the congregation. Nonetheless, she knew she had to make this decision to save herself from being completely engulfed by the demands and expectations of both Tom and the church family. It seemed to her that she had virtually sacrificed her very self for their approval and support.

Once word of her intended divorce became public, many at Jerusalem Bible Church and in her blood family pressed her to re-examine her obligations to them with appeals to her sense of loyalty and indebtedness. Some in the Christian Marriage Enrichment group gave her the impression that she had betrayed them. Prayer chains and ministry visits by others in the congregation intruded into her life and served to remind her that she was destroying the illusion of family cohesion. She was finally coaxed into reversing her decision as a result of the guilt created by her mother, brother, and pastor. Mom appealed to Marilyn's guilt and spoke of the heartache and sleepless nights the divorce was causing her. Her brother, a Sunday School Superintendent, addressed himself to how she was damaging her witness to scriptural truth. In addition, her minister, Pastor Reed, asked her to pray about her debt of loyalty to the church and the disharmony her decision was creating.

RULES

As we have just seen, Marilyn was asked to pay a high price for loyalty to her religion. She was required to sacrifice her need for autonomy and personal decision making for the sake of maintaining harmony and cohesiveness within the organizational family. Marilyn's case also helps illustrate the operation of rules and how they govern the expression of loyalty.

Every family, including that of the church, relies upon a system of rules, both stated and unstated, to help members comprehend what is permitted for themselves and others. Rules characterize, regulate, and help stabilize how families function as a unit. If a family's rules are known, that system's definition of its internal relationships can be understood.[6] In the case of righteous religion, some of the overt rules around loyalty include (1) submitting one's will and intellect to what the church teaches in regard to sound doctrine; (2) aligning oneself to the decisions of those in authority rather than relying upon one's conscience or feelings; and (3) not wandering too far from the voice of the shepherd or the safety of the flock.

Righteous religion's overt rules concerning loyalty inadvertently seem to discourage differentiation of self, which Virginia Satir believes is important for the development of a mature personality.[7] She believes that mature individuals "are able to take full charge of themselves by assuming responsibility for their own choices and decisions," trust their own perceptions, be in touch with their own feelings, and be willing "to see differentness and differentiation as a potential for growth and learning rather than as a threat."[8]

Covert rules operate in the church groups just as they do in any other family. Insofar as they are unwritten rather than explicit, they often have the force of a hidden, agreed-upon pact, existing beneath the surface, binding members to the church family in powerful, and unconscious ways. The loyalty of the faithful is reinforced by layers of unwritten rules which are interwoven into the psyche and affect judgment by tapping into guilt and fear of abandonment or exclusion.

To understand the impact of covert rules upon a person's allegiance or fidelity to the church, it is necessary to return to some examples from Marilyn's story. Loyalty to both her congregational and nuclear families, as well as guilt and fear, prompted her not to divorce her husband Tom. Five scenarios where covert rules concerning loyalty have surfaced as a result of stress in the family system are illustrated. The story is taken up below at the point where others are attempting to influence her decision.

Womens' Bible Study Member: We thought you were one of us and held the same values as we did. If you were one of us, you would respect our values and try to abide by them.

Christian Marriage Enrichment Couple: We counted on you. Hundreds of couples have counted on you. Marriage Enrichment couples don't divorce–this is a principle to which we are committed. We work things out when our marriages are in trouble. You have betrayed our ministry.

Her Brother: How will this affect your children and grandchildren's fidelity to scriptural truth? After all, marriage is the symbol of Christ's faithfulness to the church. Your decision to divorce Tom will weaken and undermine your own faith. When you pick and choose what you want to believe from scripture, you are that much closer to betraying your faith altogether.

Her Mother: Our family believes in the teachings of Holy Scripture. We don't violate by divorcing on a whim or under the pretense of moving on with our lives. I'm embarrassed to be seen in church or to explain this to my friends. Haven't I taught you better? Is this any way to repay your family for generations of fidelity?

Her Minister, Pastor Reed: I count on people like you to hold the congregation together. I am personally very hurt that you would decide to create such disunity and disharmony in our community. Marilyn, my friend, how have we failed you? We were such a happy family before you made this decision.

In undifferentiated family systems, including righteous authoritarian religion, loyalty and rules around that loyalty are rigid and binding. In Marilyn's case, the Bible Study group was quite explicit: if she wanted to be one of them, she had to adhere to their belief system and values. The Christian Marriage Enrichment couple let her know that CME couples do not divorce, and her brother upped the ante by informing her that good Christians betray scripture by seeking divorce. Her mother conveyed the rule that marital fidelity is an expected way to show gratitude to the family's religious heritage. Finally, Pastor Reed told her that a "minister" as trusted as she should not rock the boat.

The appeals to religious loyalty and the explication of the rules, overt and covert, underpinning this loyalty eventually pressured Marilyn to capitulate. She felt a deep need for finding her own voice on the one hand, and a pull toward family/church loyalty on the other. "Just as there is a strong desire to become autonomous and separate from one's family, there is an equally strong desire for closeness and attachment, and for fulfillment of loyalty obligations."[9] For Marilyn, guilt and fear of exclusion, as well as her desire to belong, won out. Thus Marilyn's need to become more fully and confidently an "I" was suffocated by the demands, rules, and expectations of the "we," "us," and "our" of the church family.[10]

Chapter 8

Spinning a Web

Families have a great investment in maintaining balance or equilibrium in their households no matter how maladaptive the system. Where fusion or enmeshment among members is high (e.g., when everyone is minding everyone else's business) and differentiation of self is low (e.g., when people have no voices of their own), members can have a difficult time finding a stable balance between needs for belonging and needs for maintaining their self-identity.[1] This conflict between seemingly divergent needs occasions tension and anxiety within a family. When a certain degree of emotional intensity is reached between members in an undifferentiated family, a third person may be triangulated in to reduce the tension and restabilize the system.[2] Such triangulation often is an attempt by one family member to elicit an ally to support her or him against another. "In the cases where the anxiety is too great for this threesome, others may become involved, forming a series of interlocking triangles. Although such triangles are usually created in an effort to achieve resolution, they actually tend to prevent resolution and the instability remains, with more family members participating in an escalating and increasingly unstable emotional field."[3] Thus, it is easy to see how such families become even more enmeshed and stuck together when the conflict is allowed to spread throughout the family and dictates the nature of familial interactions.

Authoritarian religion, much like a family, desires to sustain a sense of equilibrium (or homeostasis) within its system. Frequently, however, balancing the system involves silencing the voices of members. As we have seen, the parental church demands loyalty, uniformity of belief, and submissiveness from its members. This pressure often clashes with the needs of the children to develop an adult identity and mature personally and spiritually. Ironically, the church's effort to stabilize the system often succeeds in destabilizing it, creating the very disorder it strives to avoid. For example, in an effort to curb the influence of the gay rights lobby, a minister calls a news conference to enlist support against an antidiscrimination bill. While some people are convinced, others are offended, and even alienated. What the minister is attempting, then, is to triangle in the public, adding strength to the position of the denomination or congregation in order to offset dissenting opinion from within. In other words, he brings in outside support to stabilize the organization internally. The greater public opinion the minister gains for the anti-gay position gives the illusion of wider consensus and by extension, moral correctness. This triangulation, in turn, has the effect of encouraging group submissiveness and deflecting any minority opinions that might destabilize the system.

In the story below, the concept of triangulation is illustrated. What starts out as a conflict between two people becomes a tangle of interlocking triangles which, instead of bringing about stability in the congregation, causes increased tension, imbalance, and fragmentation.

Dean Dawson was pastor of an active and growing church. Signs of the Tabernacle Assembly's success were its long list of new members, its continual need to expand its facilities, the number of members of all ages enrolled in its ministries, and standing room only at all the services. People loved the spirit at Tabernacle Assembly and often spoke positively of the compassion of Pastor Dawson. They were attracted by the well-crafted services, relevant sermons, hospitality, and the acceptance that prevailed there.

Dissension, however, was seething below the surface of this outwardly harmonious congregation. There was growing alarm among certain members at what they termed as Pastor Dawson's "liberalism." Complaints were presented to the Board of Elders, who had called Dean Dawson to ministry at Tabernacle Assembly three years ago. The board, both distressed by and sympathetic to these concerns, called Pastor Dawson to a special meeting.

At this meeting, they told him that he was not fulfilling his ministry of preparing the faithful for spiritual warfare between

God's people and the forces of Satan. It was their belief that Pastor Dawson was not witnessing Gospel values by his "soft" positions on premarital sex, abortion, homosexuality, and social drinking. The elders objected to the fact that he didn't openly and vigorously admonish and condemn offenders in these areas. They took him to task for not upholding the inerrancy of scripture and for publicly contending that passages from Matthew's Gospel were not the authentic words of Jesus but were added later. They were particularly upset about a sermon he preached on Revelation in which, among other things, he said that the imagery should be taken symbolically or mythologically rather than literally. To tell people that there was no real beast coming out of the sea or no such thing as a dragon was, to the elders' mind, contrary to scriptural truth.

The Board of Elders unanimously recommended that Pastor Dawson take some time to "go to the Lord" and to rededicate his life to God. To reorient his ministry in the name of Jesus, the Board drew up a list of conditions that must be met within the next six months if the pastor were to continue at Tabernacle Assembly. After looking over the list, Pastor Dawson left the Board meeting feeling unjustly accused, personally and professionally violated, and determined to win as many allies to his cause as possible.

The very next day, he called a meeting of his supporters in the various ministries at Tabernacle Assembly and informed them of the Board's attempt to bring him into line. The finance committee was up in arms because they saw that his gifts and style of ministry were necessary for the continued financial success of their church. Joining the chorus of support were the Missionary Board, the Sunday School Superintendent and his teachers, and the Bread for Life Society, all of whom benefited from Pastor Dawson's dynamic leadership. The pastor encouraged all his supporters to write letters to the Board of Elders, stating that they upheld Pastor Dawson and felt his teaching reflected gospel values.

The Board had instructed Pastor Dawson to make clear statements at all services the following Sunday regarding scriptural condemnation of sex outside of marriage, abortion, and homosexuality. The pastor's tongue-in-cheek manner of making these clarifications intimated to listeners that he was more sympathetic to their difficulties with these issues than he was to the Board's concerns about orthodoxy. When the youth ministers and other church employees met, he told them the Board demanded that everyone "openly living in sin" was to resign. When the employees decided to protest at services on the following Sunday, he did nothing to stop them. Finally, when fulfilling the Board mandate to fire the Tabernacle Assembly music minister, Pastor Dawson suggested to him that he might consider taking legal action to redress his grievance.

When word of Pastor Dawson's activity reached the Board, they attempted to stabilize the situation by holding a meeting and asking for the recalcitrant pastor's resignation. When the employees and congregation of Tabernacle Assembly heard of the Boards' decision, the administrative effort to decrease the tension actually escalated it. Members of the staff called a news conference, picketed the church office under the watchful eye of television cameras, and congregation members by the dozens withheld financial support and went door-to-door encouraging others to do the same. When Pastor Dawson's successor arrived at Tabernacle Assembly to restore order and ensure scriptural inerrancy, there was such disequilibrium and chaos that he didn't know where to begin.

The tensions and stresses that give rise to triangulation are inherent in righteous religions. This is due to the emphasis in authoritarian religion on doctrinal conformity and uniformity, both of which promote an enmeshment in the family relational system. In contrast, many members in these congregations are moving toward greater maturity, autonomy, and individuation. Adults are often better informed and more independent than their own parents; the general population is more educated, reads more, and has greater access to pertinent information than previous generations; and polls show that Catholics, in particular, know that they can disagree with church teaching and remain good Catholics in their own minds. In other words, many members of authoritarian religions have given themselves permission to do their own thinking and form a spiritual connection with God in their own way. This ability to be self-directed often sets them on a course toward discovering their own voices. Likewise, it positions believers in direct opposition to righteous religion's need to keep them undifferentiated and, hence, fused to itself and to its teachings. The fragmentation that occurs when these two powerful forces collide frequently results in Christians feeling alienated, adrift, and betrayed. In order to reduce the tension and instability resulting from these clashes, both members and the leadership often attempt to gain allies to their side by means of triangulation. As can be seen from the case of Pastor Dawson, triangles beget interlocking triangles often leaving no winners and a profoundly destabilized family.

Chapter 9

Scapegoating

As we have seen in the previous chapter on triangulation, undifferentiated relational systems usually have high tension levels which results in triangulating a third entity, person, or group to reduce the stress. Examples of this were found in the conflict between Pastor Dawson and the Board of Elders. In the story that will follow, another form of tension reduction, that of displacing conflict onto a third party, will be described. Sometimes referred to as an "identified patient,"[1] this person (or persons) is the symptom bearer who externalizes and gives form to the dysfunction of the system so that other family members can appear healthy. This process is often called "scapegoating."[2]

The person who is triangulated or elected to carry the symptoms is predictable and often related to the dynamics of unresolved conflicts within the family relationship system. In enmeshed families, differences and dissension are seen as threats to the stability and continuity of the system with outspoken or oppositional children singled out for "prejudicial scapegoating."[3] "The family member who is different–whose difference betokens family disunity–becomes the victim and is punished for that difference."[4] Scapegoated people who attempt to address unresolved family conflicts are often held responsible for the very problems that they are trying to rectify. This "detouring," then, takes the spotlight off the family and refocuses it on the dissenting troublemaker.[5] Dr. Sylvia Daniels, in the following illustration, is assigned by the parental church the role of acting-out child needing discipline and therapy when she used her teaching position to tell the truth.

Sister Sylvia Daniels had been singled out by her religious order to study in Europe for a doctoral degree in theology. Her time overseas was liberating and productive. She published several articles on theological matters in scholarly journals and her dissertation was so well received that eventually it was published in book form.

When Dr. Sylvia Daniels returned from Europe, she received several teaching offers and finally accepted a position on the theology faculty of a major Catholic university. She continued to publish in theological journals on topics sufficiently orthodox and traditional that she was able to win tenure and promotion, but internally her views in relation to the church were changing. Influenced by her students and by the works of feminist theologians, she found that many things she wanted to write or teach would put her in jeopardy with the university and with her religious congregation. Increasingly, Sylvia saw the Church leadership to be guilty of misogyny and oppression of women, and she took exception to so-called male "celibates" dictating to women or men about the role of sex and sexuality in their lives.

Sylvia undertook a study of clerical sexuality with a male colleague in the psychology department. Receiving a sizable research grant from a private foundation, they were able to interview hundreds of male religious about their sexual practices. Their findings revealed much hidden genital activity and considerable confusion about sexual matters. The two researchers concluded that the church was being unfair to ask these men to speak and teach in an area where their own lived experience had been denied. Additionally, Sylvia and her co-author called for an end to clerical celibacy, inclusion of women in the priesthood, and a complete reassessment of the church's teaching on sexuality and gender.

Sylvia knew that the revelatory and dissenting nature of their book would cause controversy. Her sisters in the order and many on the university faculty tried to defend her right to academic freedom, but there were many others who attempted to persuade the board of trustees to revoke her tenure and dismiss her from the theology faculty. While Sylvia's psychologist co-writer was spared controversy, she, as a Catholic theologian, became the focus of attacks, both verbal and written. Sylvia, rather than her research findings regarding clerical sexuality, became the issue. The bishops who were interviewed by the media denied the extent of the problem and accused her of grandstanding, abusing her teaching privileges, and using her faculty position irresponsibly.

The trustees were subjected to considerable pressure from all sides. To reduce the tension, they were compelled to eliminate its source by firing Sylvia. Her religious congregation was instructed by the Vatican to seek a statement from Sylvia retracting her conclusions and to discipline her by having her refrain from writing or speaking publicly for a full year.

Sylvia's research unearthed secrets and addressed unresolved conflicts, both of which the parental church wished to keep under wraps. Furthermore, she publicly voiced dissent with the church family and thereby threatened the stability of the system. These actions produced considerable tension on the part of church and university leaders and led them to reactions of denial. Instead of addressing the problems she raised, they displaced the conflict onto the dissenter. In effect, the family scapegoated the acting-out child, making an issue of Sylvia rather than the problems she surfaced.[6] They chose to target their own child rather than facing the truths kept secret in the family.

Like other conditional parents, the church appears dedicated to keeping its members bonded to it so as to give the appearance of one, unified, like-minded family. The pursuit of this ideal leads to focusing "a great deal of energy and resources on keeping secrets"[7] and filtering out information that might damage its image. A core concern on the part of righteous authoritarian religion is to control what is open for discussion and how it is discussed in the relational system. Whenever a family member threatens to usurp this authority by surfacing secrets and bringing unresolved conflicts to the open forum, powerful forces and conspiracies arise to contain and repress the information.[8] In Sylvia's case, power and control prevailed, and the illusion of unanimity was restored by scapegoating and moving to dispossess her.

Chapter 10

Shadow Carriers

Another category of people targeted as symptom bearers in enmeshed families are those who embody the negative projections of that family. In order to stabilize the family relational system, the lack of differentiation or insistence on uniformity among the parental clerical generation leads to the expectation of this sameness in the children's generation. In this family projection process the need for sameness prevails and it is usually the most vulnerable of the deviating members who are singled out to carry the unwanted and presumably evil elements of the family.[1]

This process of projection is found in the family of righteous religions as well as in blood families. A group commonly singled out by both for the role of shadow carrier are gay men and lesbians. This phenomenon seems to emanate particularly, but not exclusively, from the male sector of the family system. Men are conditioned to give importance to and develop primarily their societally defined masculine traits, even though all humans are made up of elements of both masculinity and femininity. For many men, their non-integrated feminine side is feared, split off from awareness, and consigned to the unconscious "shadow" level. In a society that prizes only half of the masculine personality, male homosexuality is a "shadow issue," a projection of feared aspects of the self that traditionally have been disallowed in men in Judeo-Christian societies. Thus, man's feminine soul, or anima, is repressed or split-off from the self, disowned, and given to someone else, namely the gay male.[2]

A question frequently asked is why does the Catholic church, particularly the male parental members, so vehemently scapegoat gay men and lesbians (who also seem to threaten and carry the projections of the parental church but for additional reasons)? The most obvious answer is that the purportedly celibate male parental generation in a church that attempts to reject Eros and sexuality is threatened by children who are known for the nature of their sexual orientation and possible expression.[3]

Another explanation lies in the previously discussed level of emotional and psychosexual development of Roman Catholic priests. In the comprehensive psychological investigation of the American priesthood referred to in Chapter 5, it was reported that a majority of priests in the study had not achieved an integrated psychosexual identity; were functioning at a preadolescent or adolescent level of sexual development; employed an inordinate amount of energy to keep their public behavior from straying out of bounds; rationalized continued autoerotic problems as necessary outlets for their sexual energies; and put a tremendous amount of effort into adjusting to celibacy and dealing with nonintegrated sexuality.[4] One of the authors of the report pointed to frequently reported clinical findings that many church personnel "lack a clear idea of their own sexual orientation, that they are either undeveloped emotionally or that the controls of church structures have prevented them from achieving any real sense of masculinity or femininity."[5] Such undevelopment and undifferentiation yields anxiety which is often reduced by detouring or scapegoating an even more vulnerable other–in this case, the lesbian or gay man.

A final rationale to explain the church's scapegoating of gays and lesbians can be found in the emerging evidence demonstrating that a large number of people of same-gender orientation have historically chosen the priesthood.[6] Current estimates on numbers vary, with one study calculating that 40 to 60 percent of the clergy are gay, with the next generation of seminarians weighing in at 40 to 70 percent.[7] Another reliable estimate places the number of priests at 38 to 42 percent.[8] Given the significant psychosexual underdevelopment within the clerical ranks, many priests "don't even know if they're gay, or cannot admit it to themselves or others."[9] Fear of their same-gender attractions has terrified gay and lesbian individuals for centuries and, thus, it is understandable that this phenomenon would occur among the clergy as well. It is no wonder that lesbians and gays carry the shadow for the many clergy whose emotional and sexual feelings toward their own gender have been split-off, repressed, labeled as evil, and compartmentalized. In this "projective identification process," the unwanted and unconscious (or sometimes conscious) internalized evil is unloaded onto the lesbian or gay man, who then serves as a container for the disowned aspects of the self.[10] The story that follows will illustrate this phenomenon of shadow carrying.

Father Donald Smith was very pleased with the hiring of Carl Watts, a former seminarian, for the position of Diocesan Youth Director. The Diocesan Board of Religious Education (DBRE), which Father Smith chaired, had interviewed several candidates. Donald thought Carl to be head and shoulders above the rest and the Board concurred. There was something about Carl that Donald found engaging but he couldn't quite put his finger on it. Above all, he felt that Mr. Watts could do the job, and he was right.

Carl's effectiveness became immediately apparent as he traveled from parish to parish, starting and encouraging local Catholic youth groups. His training seminars for adult leaders proved successful in inspiring large numbers of lay people to devote their time and talent to youth ministry. Not only could he present well to adult audiences, but his retreats for teenagers were so popular that waiting lists were compiled. Pastors, who were initially wary of this young, charismatic outsider, were won over by the increasing numbers of teenagers and their families who attended Mass on Sunday and contributed to the collection basket.

As time went on, Father Donald and the DBRE received reports of some controversial programs that Carl was conducting. They heard that in both his leadership training seminars and youth retreats, Mr. Watts was presenting information on the special struggles of gay and lesbian teenagers in regard to suicide, substance abuse, and depression. Additionally, he held several parent education nights on the same topic during which every seat was filled. A similar seminar for priests was sparsely attended.

The brochure that accompanied the invitation to the priests' seminar made many priests question where the DBRE and especially Father Donald, its chair, stood in relation to the blatant "promotion of a homosexual life-style." Donald realized how vulnerable he was in that he had been so instrumental in hiring Carl. Donald panicked and something compelled him to disassociate himself from any taint of this homosexual issue. He decided to take up the calls of many priests to halt the spread of evil throughout the parishes by conducting his own investigation.

Donald had picked up rumors that Carl was often seen at Sunday Mass in the company of the same man and that they received communion together. He reasoned that if they were Catholic and gay that they might attend the monthly meeting of a group that serves that population. Father Smith knew that one of its members, named Scott, came to confession each Saturday afternoon to discuss his struggles with being gay and celibate. After hearing Scott's confession and giving him absolution, Donald asked Scott if he wouldn't mind answering a few questions. He inquired who attended these "outlawed meetings" and particularly if a man named Carl was often present. Scott felt doubly conflicted; first, about being confronted in the confessional and secondly, about being questioned by a man he trusted concerning a group with whom he had a bond of loyalty. He reluctantly admitted that a man named Carl attended the group and hesitantly answered questions about Carl's description, who he was with, if they were lovers, and if Carl was known to be sexually active.

Father Donald gave a report at the next meeting of the Diocesan Priests Senate in which he distanced himself from Carl by revealing Carl's homosexuality and morally reprehensible life-style. Many Senate members professed shock that the Diocesan Youth Director was a member of an organization disallowed by the bishop. Some were extremely upset that this man was living openly in "homosexual sin" while at the same time receiving the sacred Eucharist. It was Donald's impression that the issue was generating a great deal of internal emotion, but his brothers were attempting to contain themselves in priestly fashion. Eventually it was decided that the source of potential scandal must be eliminated. Donald informed his colleagues that he was taking charge of the matter by firing Carl as soon as possible.

The next morning, when Carl was ushered into his office, Father Donald was overpowered by a memory long-repressed. He suddenly knew why he initially had found Carl so engaging. The scene in his mind was of himself as a young seminarian in Rome being embraced by the only human with whom he had allowed himself sexual intimacy. His partner in the flashback was a man nearly identical in appearance to Carl.

When tension becomes high in undifferentiated or enmeshed systems, one way to reduce the pressure is to give the problem away, much like a hot potato, effectively creating a division between the righteous and the "unwashed." Carl increased the tension in the diocesan family by speaking the unspeakable and conducting retreats, seminars, and parent education nights about the troubles of gay and lesbian teenagers. The issue that Carl was opening for discussion triggered something deep inside many priests who reacted by calling for a halt to such "evil." Thus, unknowingly, Carl became a shadow carrier, bearing the feared or disowned parts of the priests' sexuality.

The projection onto Carl was an attempt to reduce the tension not only in the family system but also within the priests themselves. Such scapegoating onto the most vulnerable member is common in undifferentiated families where differences, let alone noncompliance, is not permitted. In the case of Carl's church family, "giving scandal" was the euphemism used for blowing the cover on homosexuality within the ranks of church employees. Carl's gay-affirming stance rendered him particularly vulnerable in that he defied unspoken family rules by "normalizing" a way of life that the parental church would prefer its children to see as evil and intrinsically disordered. Since intolerance toward gay men and lesbians is one of the few acceptable prejudices still condoned by the family of righteous religions, the conditions for scapegoating and disinheriting someone like Carl were in place. By allowing him to carry shadows for the parental generation, the fathers were able to return to the comfortable status quo of nonintegrated sexuality. The enemy was removed and it was no longer inside them.

Chapter 11

A Disowned Past

As has been seen in previous chapters, when tension increases in undifferentiated family systems, the strategies of triangulation and projection frequently are employed to reduce pressure. Another method of tension reduction is called "emotional cutoff" and is used by highly fused family members to gain relief from the anxiety associated with maintaining a relationship with their families.[1]

People sometimes flee emotional attachments, leaving them unresolved. This flight may take the form of physical or emotional distancing and give the fleeing person an illusion of independence. Murray Bowen has referred to this as pseudo independence in that people leaving families to avoid emotional intensity often end up in relationships that are likewise dependent, reactive, and enmeshed.[2] Bowen further suggests that the more intense the attempts at cutting off the past, the more likely it is that the recreated family will be an exaggerated version of the original family.[3] In fact, the very nature of the cutoff "is a critical determinant of how individuals handle all subsequent emotional relationships."[4]

Cutoff from the parental church occurs in much the same way as it does in families. When people flee from unresolved emotional ties, it is also quite likely, as in families, that the new relationships or allegiances will be symbolic pawns to heal the conflicts with the parental church.[5] For example, if people feel ill-treated by the Father God or unnurturing maternal religion, they often sever ties and search for more emotionally satisfying parenting in another household of faith.

The manner with which this flight takes place reflects the degree of differentiation of self from the parental church.[6] People who are more differentiated are able to think independently and clearly, and they often grieve their way out of the familial church thoughtfully and gradually. Less differentiated individuals depart more abruptly, acting more on their emotions than reason. They are easily stressed into action and any unaddressed conflict with the parental church increases their tension level such that bolting seems the only way to manage the anxiety.[7]

Additionally, the degree of emotional distancing is related to the degree of unresolved attachment individuals have with their religion.[8] People who are heavily fused with the church and for whom Christianity is intertwined with their self-definition have few boundaries with which to defend themselves from the demands for uniformity and the pressures for cohesiveness. "Should the fusion-demanding situation reach an unbearable stage, some members may seek greater distance . . . for self-preservation."[9] The following story of Antonio illustrates the phenomenon of emotional cutoff in a person who possesses a high degree of unresolved attachment to his parental church.

Antonio was his mother, Rosa's, pride and joy. On the day of his baptism, Rosa dedicated him to God in the hope that someday he would become a priest. Antonio grew up in the midst of Saint Lucy's Church and was enthusiastically devoted to helping Father Lopez serve the daily Mass. He would arrive early and get the altar and the vestments ready for the morning celebration. Father Lopez frequently referred to "Tonino" as "my right-hand man," and said he couldn't run the place without him. Antonio attended the parish grade school and loved coloring pictures of Jesus and Mary and learning the prayers of the church.

When he graduated from high school, he decided to accept a position as a bank clerk in order to provide for his mother before he entered the seminary. One day, while working in the bank, he met Sharon who was in the process of divorcing an abusive husband. They fell in love and, although she had been baptized in the New Hope Bible Church before her marriage, she was willing to attend Mass with Antonio. They began to formulate plans for marriage.

Rosa was heartbroken at the prospect of her son giving up his dream of the priesthood in order to marry a divorced woman. Father Lopez was equally distraught at having this young man he had mentored lured away from the priesthood. Furthermore, if he had to resort to marriage, did it have to be with a divorced fundamentalist? Father Lopez made it clear that he wouldn't help validate their marriage in the eyes of the church. He urged Antonio to leave Sharon and follow his vocation to the priesthood or, if he failed to do that, to marry a good Catholic girl who was not divorced.

Antonio was shocked by Father Lopez's reaction. This man who had always been so supportive was now demanding that Antonio conform by surrendering his principles and his love for Sharon. Choking with emotion, Antonio felt suffocated by the pressure to acquiesce as well as emotionally abandoned by the man he viewed as his own father. As he left, he angrily slammed the rectory door.

The following Sunday, he accompanied Sharon to the New Hope Bible Church. He was overwhelmed by the welcome he received there; it reminded him of the family feeling at St. Lucy's when he was a child. He felt as though he had come home to a true family of Christianity. Antonio eventually chose to be rebaptized and to take Jesus Christ as his Lord and Savior.

During the time that he and Sharon were preparing for their Christmas wedding, Antonio became involved with various ministries at the New Hope Bible Church. He and Sharon volunteered to be part of the Home Visitation Outreach, taking the Word of God from door to door. He liked the Bible-based certainty of his new religion where answers to life's problems were clearly given. Throughout this time of conversion, his mother prayed daily for his return to Catholicism and even sent him holy cards to remind him that the saints were doing likewise.

Several years later, Rosa died. Antonio was extremely anxious about returning to Saint Lucy's for his mother's funeral and seeing Father Lopez again. He hadn't been back to the church since the day he had angrily fled Father's office. However, he knew he had to attend the service and nervously took his place in the front row with other family members. The funeral Mass was beautiful and the choir sang his mother's favorite hymns. At first, Antonio refused to budge from his sitting position with his arms folded in front of him, but gradually he found himself kneeling as he watched the altar boy performing the familiar liturgical movements. He saw himself in the little boy, whose black hair and innocence were so much like his own when he served Mass for Father Lopez many years ago. The sights, the sounds, and smells were the same, and he found himself in tears.

Antonio grew up with Catholicism shaping his self-definition, beliefs, values, and emotional reactions. What he discovered at his mother's funeral was that he couldn't cut himself off from something that was so woven throughout the fiber of his being. When Father Lopez's demands for conformity seemed so offensive and rejecting to Antonio, he left abruptly instead of grieving the loss of a church that was so much a part of himself. His departure was an act of self-preservation and an attempt to gain independence. However, Antonio's immediate fusion with the New Hope Bible Church community was almost a replication of his involvement with Saint Lucy's. Not only was he wholeheartedly invested in his new faith family, but he also looked to it for the same sense of affirmation and belonging that he had received as a youngster at Saint Lucy's. The Bible-based church provided both the safety and certainty of his early Catholic experience, as well as an opportunity to heal the rupture caused by the betrayal Antonio felt at the hands of Father Lopez.

Antonio's experience at Rosa's funeral left him knowing how deeply bonded he was to his Catholic heritage. At some level, he realized that by severing himself he had only intensified his feelings of estrangement from the parental church. The funeral served to recall to mind nostalgic and nurturing memories of the past, and he left Saint Lucy's that day knowing that his emotional attachments to Catholicism were very much unresolved. Cutting off and disowning an important part of his past was not possible; somehow it had to be integrated with the present.

Chapter 12

Don't Rock the Boat

Every system, including the family and authoritarian religion, has "internal, ongoing, sustaining, dynamic interactional processes"[1] that are ongoing and help assure homeostasis or balance. These processes help systems to weather stress, cope with drastic changes, and provide stability. Regardless of how dysfunctional, a family will strive to maintain a status quo simply because it is known, predictable, and family members have regularly made their accommodations to it. The same forces that maintain the homeostatic balance are also stubbornly resistant to change, so much so that virtually anything that threatens to create disequilibrium is made subordinate. In other words, the system as it has been constituted and defined must be preserved at all costs, and some families will go to any extreme to restore equilibrium.

A "good enough" family, however, will not have to go to extraordinary lengths to accommodate change since its flexibility allows adaptation to evolving circumstances and to the developmental needs of its members. The rules that describe the patterns of communication and direct what can and cannot occur between members are generally adaptable and resilient. The rules tend to be overt and explicit, which provides for open negotiation about differences, problems, and even the very process of rule-making itself. They also permit a continuous, "free exchange of information within a family and between the family and the outside world."[2] This feedback serves as a self-correcting mechanism, enabling the family to survive, remain stable, and re-establish homeostasis in a functional, dynamic way.

The following story about Liberty Fellowship illustrates how threatening change can be in a problematic system and how a church family can put preservation of the status quo above all else.

The story tells how an entrenched group within the congregation is confronted with disequilibrium. Lacking the resiliency to assimilate differences and accommodate change, Liberty Fellowship returned to a former way of operating which, while comfortable for some, disenfranchised many others.

Pastor Ronald Jordan considered himself fortunate to be pastor of Liberty Fellowship for the past eighteen years. It was the only Bible-based church in the small town of Springdale and many of the prominent citizens were members. The old families had worked hard and had succeeded in paying off the debts accrued by renovating the church and building a fellowship hall and office complex. Rather than electing representatives to advise the Board of Elders, Pastor Jordan simply appointed the people who had been loyal to Liberty Fellowship over the years and who had exercised leadership in Vacation Bible School, the Missionary Society, the Revival Planning Committee, and the Mens Prayer Breakfast Group. The members were good friends, frequently socialized together, and agreed on most matters. Since Pastor Jordan wanted the monthly church board meetings to be harmonious and congenial, he kept the same advisory group for ten years. It, in effect, constituted his only means of gaining information about the congregation.

With the escalating price of land and the problems of urban dwelling, Springdale began to attract commuters who worked in the city across the river. These were often young couples with families who found the small town a favorable place to raise their children. At first Liberty Fellowship welcomed the new arrivals and appreciated the fresh faces and the additional income. Gradually this new group started networking and formed their own Bible study and prayer groups. Out of these gatherings emerged a number of ministries for youth discipleship, family worship, and outreach to the poor.

To some of the old-timers, it seemed that the newcomers were taking over services with their noisy children, raucous music, handholding, and even clapping. Some were heard to say such things as: "This isn't a prayer service anymore; it's a rock concert." The food bank became a problem when the homeless began showing up at all hours for handouts of food. One even scared Mrs. Schmidt, the wife of a Board member, who found what she described as a scruffy vagrant sleeping by the church door when she came for the 10:00 a.m. Women's Bible Study meeting.

At the next elders' council meeting, Mr. Schmidt brought with him a list of suggestions which he had elicited from the other members. He told the group that these recommendations were the best way to put the congregation back on an even keel and to address the growing discontent at Liberty Fellowship. Having no way to obtain feedback from a fuller representation of the members, Pastor Jordan was left to rely on the advice of his friends on the Board. From their perspective, the once tranquil congregation was getting out of hand and becoming increasingly unruly. Pastor Jordan, who always chose the path of least resistance, concurred and approved their proposal. At the service the following Sunday, Mr. Schmidt read the new rules at Liberty Fellowship. They outlawed secular or popular music, as well as clapping and hand-holding at services, and demanded closure of the church's food bank, directing all those seeking assistance to the Salvation Army Center in the city across the river.

The influx of newcomers invaded the orderly and comfortable system at Liberty Fellowship, disturbing the status quo and creating unrest. The disequilibrium threatened the longtime members who saw their consistent and predictable environment being eroded. The congregation had almost no way to accommodate change given that the Board, the primary mechanism for feedback and input in the organization, was composed entirely of like-minded individuals with little ability or need to see beyond their side of a question. These people held the power at Liberty Fellowship and functioned as a parental generation of "rule makers." They operated such that there was no way for newly arrived family members to negotiate differences. In effect, this arrangement treated the other members like stepchildren, with their needs being subordinated to those of the parental generation. When the outsiders began to rock the boat, the elders were determined to restore stability and equilibrium at all costs in the belief that their decisions were the best means for preserving the church family. The board's actions resulted in many individuals feeling alienated, cut-off, and unwanted. Desiring to be fully accepted into the family of Liberty Fellowship, these members were left with the sense that some were "natural" children more favored by the parents, whereas they were merely tolerated.

Chapter 13

Caught in the Middle

Every system has boundaries which are "rules defining who participates and how."[1] In healthy families, these well-established transactional patterns are flexible enough to provide a balance between stability on the one hand, and the growing developmental needs of its members on the other. Thus, a dynamic equilibrium operates in such families, adapting to the changing needs of individuals while at the same time maintaining the continuity of the system. Healthy families possess the quality of flexibility which is demonstrated by a natural way of intrafamily relating and an instinctive, as opposed to a rule-bound, response to problem solving. Perhaps residing at the heart of this flexibility is a respect for the views of each member and an openness to negotiate, accommodate, and experiment as circumstances warrant.

The manner in which the authoritarian religion is organized lacks this adaptability and openness. In an effort to preserve its continuity and stability, the balance has been tilted away from the needs of the children toward the authority of the parents. In so doing, righteous religion can once again be seen as a conditional parent, stifling the voices of some of its children, often refusing to negotiate over opposing views of family members, and frequently promoting a climate of opposition rather than a spirit of affiliation and affirmation within the family.[2] Such parenting often breeds alienation and leaves people feeling disillusioned in their own religious home.

Conditional parents and their offspring seldom have an easy exchange of communication since the invisible boundaries between them limit the amount and kind of contact allowed. The rules defining who participates and how are fairly "rigid and are not altered to fit the demands of a given situation."[3] When the boundaries between subsystems in a family are impermeable, neither the parents nor the children are able to cross into each other's world.[4] In the illustration that follows, a Catholic bishop will be seen struggling in what Virginia Satir terms a "closed system." Her quotation serves to summarize the story.

> Dysfunctional families constitute a "closed system": closed systems are those in which every participatory member must be very cautious about what he or she says. The principal rule seems to be that everyone is supposed to have the same feelings, opinions, and desires, whether or not this is true. In closed systems honest self-expression is impossible, and if it does occur, the expression is viewed as deviant, or "sick" or "crazy" by the . . . family. Differences are treated as dangerous; a situation that results in one or more members having to figuratively "be mad at themselves" if they are to remain in the system. The limitations placed on individual growth and health in such a group are obvious. . . . [5]

It seemed to Bishop Lucas Hill that his job had become increasingly more difficult since he was ordained bishop fifteen years ago. He was appointed the spiritual leader of his Midwestern diocese by Pope Paul VI. He recalled those early years as a time when a greater openness to a range of opinions existed and he felt free to speak his mind. Lucas remembered with fondness his superior at the time, Archbishop Rose, and how comfortably they were able to negotiate differences and cooperate on issues where they disagreed.

But now Bishop Hill felt the system had only one way of doing business and that was from the top down. Some days it seemed that his main responsibility was to accept directives from Rome and pass them on to the people of God in his diocese. Likewise, he felt pressured to act counter to his natural collaborative instincts by treating differences as dangerous and aggressively disciplining dissenting priests and laity. Previously, he had the experience of being part of a team and felt a sense of mutuality with the leadership in Rome, but now virtually his only communication with his superiors was in the form of directives or instructions to be promulgated in his diocese.

Bishop Hill, in recent years, found himself put into many untenable positions by Vatican statements that he privately considered extreme and adversarial. His job was to publicly defend these positions to the media and he often felt like hiding when the Vatican once again dug in its heels on issues such as birth control, ordination of women, married priests, and homosexuality. Lucas knew eventually a reporter would ask him to explain the official position on an issue and he would feel caught, having to be cautious, measuring his every word, and nuancing his public statements so as to appear both acceptable to the Vatican watchdogs and true to his own conscience. More and more, he found this a difficult balancing act, since the rules about who participates in the church family system and how they are to participate were becoming more rigid and non-negotiable.

Bishop Lucas, as he was fondly called by many of his priests and people, was deeply troubled about the priest shortage in the diocese and the stressful effects this had on the remaining clergy. At the same time, a group of married priests from the CORPUS organization (National Association for Married Priesthood) had volunteered to assist in rural parishes where Sunday Mass was no longer a regular occurrence. Additionally, at one of his monthly consultation sessions with the laity, several women and married men had told him of their calls by God to ordination. Yet, in spite of the serious need for priests, Bishop Hill knew there was no way that the present church would negotiate the inclusion of these willing and loyal participants into the priesthood.

Thus, it was with these and other concerns that he attended the next meeting of the National Conference of Catholic Bishops. The subject of priestly vocations was one of the main items on the agenda and Bishop Lucas particularly wished to discuss it from the viewpoint of resigned priests and the ordination of women and married men. When he attempted to do so, he was told that the topic of vocations would be addressed from only two perspectives (1) the breakdown of the family and the materialistic attraction of American Society; and (2) the overly permissive and secularized nature of seminary training. He was also informed that the questions he raised had been closed to discussion. When he attempted to press his views further, Bishop Hill was told by the Roman-trained conference secretary, pointing to the agenda, that "In the Vatican, we say *res nostra agitur*–this is our business." Lucas knew enough to shut up at this point lest he be branded as a troublemaker and scapegoated accordingly. He was angry at himself for his cowardice, however, since he had silenced his voice for political expediency.

Although many of Bishop Lucas' peers privately supported him for his outspoken stance, he, nevertheless, spent the days during the meeting feeling quite discouraged about the lack of an honest public forum wherein the true problems facing the church family could be negotiated. He sat through the remainder of the conference feeling powerless and compromised as the discussion shifted from "vocations" to questions of holy days of obligation and Peter's Pence. Lucas felt especially trapped and used as he returned home, having to report about worldly seminarians, the continuation of largely ignored holy days, and contributions to the papal purse when his priests and people were struggling with far more serious matters. Again he felt pulled between the authority of the parental generation and the genuine needs of the other generations in the family. Bishop Hill felt violated, ineffectual, isolated, and angry at both himself and the system. For the first time in his distinguished career, Lucas considered resigning.[6]

The story of Bishop Lucas Hill illustrates how a system's tendency to maintain its homeostasis can be taken to an extreme when an emphasis is placed more on stability and continuity as opposed to adaptation to changing needs. Bishop Hill desired to open for discussion some of these needs, but was blocked by the inflexibility and rigidity of the boundaries between the parental generation who made the rules concerning who participates and the nature of that participation in the family. Over the years, he had been feeling increasingly impotent and isolated as he realized how impenetrable the walls between his superiors and himself had become. On the other hand, it seemed he had no personal space or thought of his own that could not be transgressed by what he called "those Vatican watchdogs."

From a family systems viewpoint, Lucas was being engulfed by forces and rules that had him enmeshed to the extent that his feelings, opinions, and desires were expected to be in step with those of every other family member. In fused families, the boundaries downward are so permeable that parents attempt to control nearly every aspect of their children's lives, while the boundaries upward are so impermeable that children virtually have no way to communicate openly with their parents. Perhaps Lucas' discouragement, exhaustion, and anger were at least partially due to his being seen and treated as a child by the fathers of the church, while being viewed as a member of the parental generation by the people and priests under his care.

Like so many priests and bishops, Lucas wanted "good enough" parenting from the church fathers. Instead, he received conditional parenting with inclusion and approval dependent upon the acceptability of his stated opinions and behavior. In the same vein, Lucas strived to be a good parent, keeping the lines of communication between himself and his children open so they would not feel as emotionally isolated and unsupported as he did. Having listened to the stories of their hearts, he tried to negotiate on their behalf but the closed nature of the system and the inflexibility of boundaries to accommodate change left Lucas feeling caught in the middle.

Chapter 14

Business as Usual

Feedback is a "regulatory mechanism by which a system manages to maintain homeostasis, while at the same time monitoring its attempts to achieve certain of its goals. . . ."[1] In healthy families, feedback serves to exchange information and energy between people and parts of the system and between the system itself and the environment. Likewise, feedback can challenge outworn or erroneous rules, perceptions, values, and attitudes and thus help correct the family's course of action.[2]

Feedback can be manipulated to either increase or decrease any deviation in the family system.[3] The limited use of feedback to reduce change and reinforce stability was demonstrated in the previous stories of the Liberty Fellowship Board of Elders and of Bishop Hill. In the first of these examples, the flow of information was so restricted that the needs of the newly arrived members at Liberty Fellowship were not accommodated. In Bishop Lucas' case, the input at the Bishops' conference was blatantly controlled and resulted in a constriction of the family system as well as the people in it. In both cases, people who were thought to be family members felt left out and alienated.

In the following story of Pastor Kenneth Sherman, the importance of feedback as an essential element in a living, ongoing system is illustrated. With input to the parental generation virtually nonexistent, the family at Harvest Assembly was left with no self-corrective mechanisms, ways to assimilate change, or means of negotiating differences across the hierarchical boundaries of the family.

Pastor Kenneth Sherman had been a minister for thirty-eight years and was finding the demands of running his congregation more difficult with the passage of years. His arthritis was acting up more frequently and some Sunday and Wednesday evenings it took all of his energy just to go out after dinner and celebrate the worship and praise services. Everything about the ministry seemed to be more demanding than in the old days before all the changes in society had occurred. He felt that it was his duty to maintain control of all aspects of the congregation; after all, this was why he had been called as pastor of Harvest Assembly.

Keeping track of the bills, insurance, and financial needs of the church was taking up more of his time. The job seemed to require more paperwork than before and wading through each day's mail was an arduous task. He knew many of his friends in the ministerial association felt the same way and that they were envious of pastors who had large staffs to help shoulder some of the work load.

As a young preacher he used to enjoy mingling with the congregation after worship service or having an occasional dinner in one of their homes. Now he largely kept his distance because they always seemed to want something new at Harvest Assembly. In fact, this was why he started a pastor's advisory committee (in name only) and never activated it, for fear the group would meet and stir up activities for him to manage.

Pastor Sherman had developed a line of defense between himself and the people. Those coming to the door were met by Vivian, his wife for the last forty-five years. Those calling him on the phone were greeted by his loyal secretary, Marge, who prided herself on handling all matters, except those related to his fellow ministers or his children. Mrs. Wagner, a volunteer, competently looked after all educational programs for children, youth, and adults. These three women helped him to keep stability in the congregation and to free him for what he considered to be his major responsibilities of preaching the Gospel, keeping up the physical plant, and assuring financial accountability.

Over the years, church members either individually or in groups had tried to obtain his permission to begin organizations or ministries that they felt would benefit Harvest Assembly. They were usually unsuccessful, most often being intercepted by one of the three women who guarded his privacy. When congregation members were able to schedule a face-to-face meeting, the encounter consisted of their presenting the request, his denying it, and then spending the remainder of the session explaining how hard it was to run a church anymore, and how old and tired ministers like himself were getting. On several occasions, efforts were mounted to withdraw his call to ministry at Harvest Assembly but these were deflected by a solid core of members who liked the status quo.

Gradually, people stopped asking Pastor Sherman for changes. Most of the long-term members of the church were fond of their pastor and did not have the heart to ask for his resignation, especially in these later years of his ministry. Some had come to accept the ongoing inertia and stability of Harvest Assembly, while others—particularly younger members—went elsewhere, sometimes to a different fellowship entirely. Some even started their own fellowships while others stopped going to church altogether.

In an effort to preserve homeostasis or balance at Harvest Assembly, Pastor Sherman fostered few forums for information exchange. Due to his own diminishing energy level and the limited vision of his role as a pastor, he restricted feedback that would require any output of activity on his part or which would create instability for himself or, by extension, the church family. In order to preserve equilibrium at Harvest Assembly, he established rigid, non-permeable boundaries between the generations so that new information would not be allowed to generate disruption or uncertainty. By restricting input and information, Pastor Sherman was not required to redefine his goals, roles, and responsibilities and was never forced to let go of the control he envisioned as essential to maintaining homeostasis within the Assembly.

Entropy is a phenomenon wherein a certain amount of energy is unavailable for useful work. In a closed system such as Harvest Assembly, the pastor's restriction of feedback and information flow promoted an entropic situation where there was more congregational energy unavailable than available for organizational use.[4] Because members had nowhere to direct that energy at Pastor Sherman's church, they felt stifled. Some felt cut-off and stopped going to church entirely, while others remained in the stagnant environment of Harvest Assembly. Those who wanted something more went elsewhere to participate in a dynamic, spirited organization.

Because "exchange of information is essential to all living, ongoing systems,"[5] its absence can result in an organization that is robotic, overly ritualistic, legalistic, mechanical and lifeless.[6] This was certainly becoming the case as Harvest Assembly conducted business as usual.

Chapter 15

Speaking with Forked Tongue

As has been discussed, awareness of emotional enmeshment in a family is key to appreciating how its relationships work. Likewise, recognizing the various means used to maintain homeostasis is crucial to appreciating how systems operate. So also, knowing how messages are transmitted is essential to understanding how communication works within a family system. Communication takes place on at least two levels: the overt or surface level, and the nonverbal or metacommunication level, which provides additional meaning to the message on the first level. For example, someone asking "How are you?" with an expression of utter disinterest is communicating an incongruent or contradictory set of messages. In "good enough" families, the majority of messages transmitted by parents to their offspring are clear and reasonably congruent on both the overt and covert level.[1] Thus, children are not left to guess what the rules are and what is on the minds of their parents.

In families where there is conditional parenting, the messages are mixed and what is said and how it is said often is contradictory. Children hear one thing and yet sense another, frequently without being able to verbalize the discrepancy. Such offspring may experience disorientation without conscious awareness of what is causing the confusion. Mixed parental messages place children in an untenable position because the offspring usually lack permission to comment on the apparent contradictions even if they are skilled enough to do so. Additionally, they need their parents for survival, and thus have no option but to stay. Bound tightly to their parents, children in conditional families face an array of inconsistent messages, both spoken and unspoken, as well as inevitable punishments for heeding one message while disregarding its contradictory counterparts.[2]

The conditional and often alienating parental style of righteous religion mirrors this pattern. As we have seen, an intense relationship exists between Christians and their churches, which is not unlike the bonding between parents and children. Many members have internalized the church's admonitions to obey it above all else and to rely on its teaching and wisdom for guaranteed spiritual survival. In this regard, the parental generation provides its faithful children with few avenues of escape, intimating that there is neither happiness nor salvation apart from their particular interpretation of theology. In this enmeshed, inescapable familial context, members of authoritarian religions are exposed repeatedly to a series of contradictory messages and commands.

As was seen in earlier chapters, adult children in closed systems are not allowed to comment on, confront, or clarify substantive issues without encountering reprisal or reprimand. Thus, without a viable and effective process for challenging theological discrepancies, many Catholics and Fundamentalists (in spite of the fact that Fundamentalist churches purport to have democratic forms of governance) learn to expect mixed messages from their parental churches. Some become so accustomed to the repeated contradictions that they barely notice them, while others are left deeply confused, fragmented, and disillusioned. The following story illustrates the experience of one Catholic as she deals with an array of disparate messages. On one level, Madge hears overt rules and expectations from church fathers while on a second level, she is aware of covert and accompanying metacommunications.

This was Madge's first year of directing the Confirmation program at St. Catherine's parish. She was enthusiastic about instructing this group of high school juniors and seniors and was eager to transmit to them the faith that had formed her and guided her life. Madge was baptized as a Catholic and had grown to love the church. She knew since it was run by human beings it was not perfect, but, like most Catholics, she was oblivious to the amount of "doublespeak" emanating from the parental generation until after she went to work at St. Catherine's.

Madge's best friend, Lois, was secretary at the parish and one day at lunch began telling Madge some of the things she had observed or heard the local priests discussing over the years. Whenever a controversial event arose (such as a proclamation from Rome or a wayward priest who made newspaper headlines), the clergy made repeated phone calls to each other and talked often until they arrived at a version of the story that either would not upset or scandalize the laity or put themselves at odds with the church hierarchy. Lois had heard the priests trying to sanitize sermons on "hot" topics such as birth control and divorce so as not to offend people and thus affect financial contributions. She told Madge about women being praised from the pulpit and underpaid in the parish; she described priests giving homilies on justice and compassion while these same clergy gossiped viciously about brother priests they suspected of being gay.

These things set Madge to thinking and observing the church from a closer vantage point. What had only been vague awareness to her for years became more and more clear. She began to look at the teachings of the church and how it instructed its members in those beliefs. One day, Madge prepared a class on Christian principles for her confirmation students, and the discrepancies she discovered shocked her. In many cases, it seemed that the church was providing a congruent and clear message, but in others, the contradictions between what was said and what was practiced became all too apparent. She thereupon set about compiling the following list of discrepancies.

Contradictions in Catholic Teachings

Stated Principles	*Underlying Messages*
Women are to be treated with equality in the church/	. . . but they can't be priests.
Speak your truth with honesty and courage/	. . . but don't make the hierarchy look wrong. . . . but don't dissent in public. . . . but don't acknowledge disagreement among the parental generation.
"You are all children of God through faith in Christ Jesus" (Galatians 3:26)/	. . . but some children count more than others.

Stated Principles	Underlying Messages
Sex is a gift from God, a cause for celebration/	. . . but celibacy is a better gift.
Respect other religions/	. . . but the Catholic church has more truth.
Don't use birth control/	. . . but we know you do; just don't tell us about it.
Good Catholics go to Mass on Holy Days/	. . . but we won't discuss the fact that this is largely ignored.
Good Catholics go to confession regularly/	. . . but we won't discuss the fact that this is largely ignored.
Good Catholics do not masturbate/	. . . but we won't discuss the fact that this is largely ignored.
Good Catholics are pro-life/	. . . but we won't discuss the fact that this is largely ignored.
Good Catholics don't divorce/	. . . but we won't discuss the fact that this is largely ignored.
Blessed are the merciful/	. . . but some people do not deserve mercy until they repent their evil ways.
Love your enemies, do good to those who oppose you/	. . . but it's okay for the paster to speak maliciously against those who dissent from the authentic and consistent teaching of the Catholic church.
You cannot serve God and money. Where your treasure is, there also will your heart be/	. . . but it's okay to have two collections on many Sundays.
Do not judge so that you may so not be judged/	. . . but it's okay to judge abortionists, "perverts," pornographers, people in second marriages, parents who do not have their children baptized, prostitutes, and homosexuals.
Seek first the kingdom of God and God's justice, and all things will be given to you/	. . . but it's okay to be petty, ambitious, self-seeking, and jealous if you're striving to be a bishop.

.

Compiling this list impressed upon Madge the need to be a more congruent truth-teller than the parental church. It made her wonder to what extent she as a teacher and an "adult" Catholic was participating in sending mixed messages to the younger generation. With this in mind, she began the next class by sharing her list of discrepancies and inviting the students to express any mixed messages they may have received from herself, other church authorities, or the institution itself. She next followed this sharing session with a series of discussions concerning how to keep faith alive in the midst of such an apparently contradictory and alienating system.

To help her students see reality more clearly and develop their own voices of truth, Madge decided to conduct a discussion of mixed messages in the church family. In doing so, she was breaking one of the cardinal rules of a closed system, namely, don't talk about what's really happening. By surfacing the metacommunication, or the communication about the communication, she brought discrepancies to the conscious level and transmitted the clear and congruent messages characteristic of "good enough" parenting. Thus, both Madge and the students were able to give expression to that which they had vaguely sensed and to deal with these discrepancies in a much more mindful and honest way.

Chapter 16

Challenges to the Power Structure

Power, that is, "influence, authority, and control over an outcome,"[1] is a property of every system. How this power is distributed differs from family to family and "has to do with authority (who is the decision maker) and responsibility (who carries out the decision)."[2] In "good enough" families, power is lateral in that it is shared and appropriately collaborative. Parents still have the major responsibility "for child rearing, nurturance, guidance, limit setting, and discipline,"[3] but interact with their offspring in such a way as to persuade rather than coerce, invite rather than demand. In such families, children are strengthened in their capacities for decision making and self-direction.

Conversely, in conditionally parented families, power is held tightly in the hands of parents. Children are not allowed to reach their developmental potential, that is, to act and speak as adults when in fact they have reached chronological adulthood. This process of disempowerment, while seldom articulated, is often sensed by the younger generation as alienating, nonvalidating, and violating. Power is vertical in these closed families, with parental decisions narrowly delineating the parameters in which children are to function. Such offspring are to respond with unquestioning obedience and adhere to strictly defined limits. Three conditions, however, can undermine the top-down power of conditional parents: acting-out children, cross-generational alliances, and secrets.

Sometimes, children cannot conform to parental expectations and are unable to find a collaborative means within the family to seek resolution. They feel stuck, powerless, and voiceless in a system designed to keep them under control and limited in their ability to be self-directive. Often such offspring "act out" simply because they see no other viable means to express themselves.[4] Acting-out behaviors, sometimes referred to as symptoms, operate to challenge the family's power distribution in an effort to balance that power more evenly. Behaviors such as running away, withdrawing in silence, using drugs, or throwing temper tantrums allow children to control family relationships for a time. Usually the situation ends with the parents arrogating more power to themselves, thus trying to restore the family system to its original homeostasis. This parental reclaiming of the executive position in the hierarchy doesn't end the struggle between the generations, but rather, sets up a cycle wherein children again act out, parents retrench, and the power struggle continues.

Power is not distributed in quite the hierarchical, top-to-bottom fashion as family members would like to believe, however. Ordinary familial power struggles can become complicated and muddled when cross-generational coalitions or alliances are formed. For example, if parents or grandparents are more aligned with the children than with each other, the power is dispersed and the family is adrift.[5] Also, some children grow powerful by learning to manipulate the system and forming convenient alliances with the adults. Others, unfortunately, get trapped in the power struggles and end up feeling psychologically unprotected and alienated.

Secrets are an integral part of conditionally parented families and work alongside coalitions to fragment the power. "Secrets in the family system lead to conspiracies which are laden with power. A conspiracy to maintain a family secret is inherently powerful because the conspirators are then able to decide who and what is open for discussion in the family."[6] Secrets surrounding such issues as alcoholism, incest, a sibling's sexual orientation, financial irregularities, extramarital affairs, or an illegitimate child create factions in terms of who knows and who doesn't know the secret. Those "in the know" have the power and are powerfully united in the keeping of that secret.

The sharing of power is characteristic of "good enough" families. Rather than collaborating, however, conditional parents attempt to keep the power to themselves by making most of the decisions and thereby creating the conditions for disillusionment. Quite often this vertical distribution of power is upset or challenged by children seeking their voice, by parents or grandparents who align themselves with the children (or vice versa), or by secrets that redirect the power away from the parental generation.

Righteous religion holds power tightly. The parental generation requires unquestioning obedience from its children, who in turn attempt to have their voices heard. The generations frequently engage in power struggles, with the leadership striving to retain control and the members attempting to empower themselves. These tugs of war often do not follow generational lines but, from time to time, involve a crossing of generational boundaries. Examples of such crossovers include the large number of Catholic priests siding with the laity on the issue of birth control or nuns aligning with lay women against the church fathers. Secrecy abounds in this church family, often focusing on issues of sexuality (gay priests and bishops, romances and affairs, arrests, pedophilia), finances (misappropriation of funds, gambling, theft), and various addictions. The holders of these secrets can be seen as conspirators who have the power to influence outcomes. It is these traders of secrets more than the parents themselves that determine who and what is open for discussion in the family.

Father Mark had been in love with Beth since his days at Good Shepherd. He was a newly ordained priest and she was the parish secretary. For the past ten years, they had spent their vacations and his days off together. Over time, they met other couples like themselves and friends introduced them to their friends. Quietly, their partnership became an accepted reality and a cherished secret among a growing circle of parishioners both at Good Shepherd and Holy Names, where Mark was later assigned as pastor.

Somehow, though word traveled through the parish and the priestly community, it eventually arrived at the bishop's doorstep.

Bishop Singer first consulted with his advisors and then had his secretary make an appointment for Father Mark. In that meeting, the bishop told Mark that if he wanted to remain as pastor of Holy Name, he had to meet two conditions: (1) immediately sever all ties with Beth and discontinue any form of communication with her now and in the future; and (2) report to an out-of-state psychiatric facility for a two-week, comprehensive psychological evaluation followed by a possible six-month stay for "treatment." Without hesitation, Father Mark rejected the two conditions, asserted his intention to remain at Holy Name, and marched out of Bishop Singer's office.

The next day, a Saturday, Mark received a registered letter from the bishop, restating the two conditions and making it clear that if he didn't comply, he was to leave the parish immediately. Mark knew that by Monday he would be gone from Holy Name and that his last chance to speak out would be at the Masses on Sunday. At every liturgy the following day, Mark introduced Beth and told the people how positively she had influenced his ministry; being with her over the years had helped him to be a more compassionate and understanding pastor, enabling him to identify more closely with his parishioners' struggles and concerns. He took the opportunity to describe the loneliness of celibacy and appealed to the people to speak out and support life-giving relationships for their priests. He made it clear that he intended to remain with Beth for as long as God gave them years together and he told them of his pain, knowing that the decision would cost him his priestly faculties.

Responding both to his words and his history of effective ministry, the people at every Mass gave him a standing ovation. Except for a small group who felt scandalized by Father Mark's disclosure and the breaking of his celibacy vows, most people were heartbroken to learn that their beloved pastor was leaving the next day. Groups of them banded together to conduct an all-night vigil in front of the church to demonstrate their support for him and other priests who were struggling with celibacy.

That week, Bishop Singer asked the members of the priests' senate for their opinion concerning "the Father Mark affair." The reaction of the priests to this question surprised the bishop, who had expected them to give him routine support. Some outrightly sided with Mark in his opposition to celibacy, others stated that they didn't know enough about the situation to respond, while a minority supported the bishop in his exercise of power and authority.

One member of the group, who supported the bishop, was named pastor at Holy Name. He had been issued the mandate to restore order to the parish and to eliminate the reminders of that scandal. One of his first official acts was to remove the photograph of Father Mark from the pastors' gallery in the parish center which had been constructed during Mark's assignment there. The new pastor seriously underestimated the extent of Father Mark's imprint upon the parish and how deeply he was networked throughout the Holy

Name community. When word of the picture's removal spread throughout the parish, collections dropped drastically.

The story of Father Mark illustrates several of the dimensions of power and how it operates in vertically oriented family systems like religious congregations. Many clergy are failing to find a collaborative means within the family to seek resolution on the celibacy issue and are therefore responding as did Father Mark. By acting on their best intuition, they are thereby challenging the power alignment in the system. The confrontation often initiates a cycle wherein the parental generation attempts to reestablish its executive position. This forces the growing children to stand up on their own behalf, which in turn necessitates a countermove from the parents. Mark refused to give in to this power struggle but, instead, chose to lose his priestly faculties and his parish rather than relinquish Beth.

Cross-generational alliances made it difficult for Bishop Singer and Father Mark's successor at Holy Name to exercise unilateral power. In the first instance, when the bishop went before his fellow priests to garner support against Mark, the acting-out child, he found some of the priestly parents in the family aligned with Mark and his struggles with celibacy. This lack of support diluted the bishop's power, in effect delivering to him a no-confidence vote on his own generational level. The new pastor's power was also weakened by the strong coalitions that Mark and Beth had formed with parishioners. This networking across generational boundaries within the Holy Name family served to undermine the vertically oriented parental power. Children were used to sharing the power with the parent at Holy Name and were not about to give it up, especially when the new pastor tried to establish a vertical power hierarchy by removing the picture of a former, beloved parent. After all, these parishioners were the same children who had aligned themselves with Father Mark in keeping his secrets, thus being doubly empowered. Not only did they have the power that comes from being a co-conspirator, but they were also collaborators with the father in decision making in the Holy Name family. The experience left a number of alienated Christians—those who felt abandoned by Father Mark's departure, and others who felt their voices stifled by the new pastor's top-down and unilateral exercise of power.

PART THREE:
CLAIMING YOUR OWN VOICE

Chapter 17

Grieving Illusions

It is natural for believers to transfer onto Fundamentalism and Catholicism some of the expectations that they once held concerning their parents. In this regard, members innocently come to hope and trust that religion will help assuage their anxieties, convince them that the universe is welcoming to them, and reward their involvement with spiritual delight and wonder.[1] Such individuals invest a great deal of confidence and loyalty in their parental churches. Yet, as previous chapters have demonstrated, embedded within the legitimate expectations of believers reside numerous assumptions that prove to be illusory.

As people begin to glimpse the incongruity between the idealized parental church and the church as it actually is, they often become disillusioned. In the process of this discouragement, however, a more authentic or real self often emerges.[2] With the "masklike persona"[3] or false self revealed, many of the foundational presumptions, beliefs, and illusions of righteous religions are questioned or even dismembered. Once this unmasking has begun, individuals come face to face with the reality of authoritarian religion. Thus, it will be through a process of deconstructing their illusions and grieving their losses that the real self is uncovered and a personal voice claimed.

GRIEVING ILLUSIONS

For some Christians, the journey toward disillusionment has been a long course of erosion with one expectation after another slowly wearing away. For others, some event may cause a sudden, devastating awareness of the erroneous nature of their illusions about religion. In any case, a loss process has been initiated.

The first instinct of Fundamentalists and Catholics who have bonded deeply with the church is to disbelieve the evidence they are seeing about the parental church.[4] Some may question if they are losing their religion. Most try in some way to protect themselves from this threatening awareness; they simply cannot believe that many of their assumptions about God and their religion are untrue. Along with this disbelief, there is often confusion, disorientation, and sometimes even numbness.

Humans can handle only so much disillusionment at once and attempt to buffer themselves against the full magnitude of loss. Some try to hang on to their beliefs and illusions with all their strength while others try to cut their losses and move on. Those who tend to hold on often devalue their own perceptions by denying there is a problem, or convincing themselves that they are blowing things out of proportion. They may attempt repeatedly to rationalize away the humanness of the institution and its representatives. It is not uncommon for them to hop from church to church or pastor to pastor searching for an experience that will keep alive their earlier expectations about parental religion. In their bargaining, some redouble their efforts at being good Christians, while pining for the good old days when the church seemed to be a good and honest parent.

"Like holding-on efforts, letting-go behaviors protect people from being overcome by the magnitude of their losses and help them manage the pain of losing something or someone that was once cherished."[5] Individuals in the midst of disillusionment find themselves painfully alternating between holding on/letting go positions. Those more disposed to letting go may believe they have been deceived by the church, poorly parented, and sold a false bill of goods. They may deny that their religious community was ever important to them by accentuating the negative in the institution and demeaning everything either Bible-based or Catholic, while those who hold on to their faith may over-idealize it. People who engage in letting-go strategies tend to devalue their religious heritage per-haps even to the point of "bashing" it at every opportunity. The temptation here is to summarily cut themselves off from the church much like Antonio did in Chapter 11.

People feel the full extent of their disenchantment when all attempts to hold on to their illusions about righteous religions or their efforts to exorcise the parental church from their lives no longer work. Catholics and Fundamentalists who had once bonded deeply with their religion now see it unmasked, shorn of illusions, and with secrets exposed. They realize that the church is no longer able to protect or guide them, and they may feel deceived or even betrayed. With their illusions and belief system in disarray, they perceive no "hope for reclaiming what is gone, returning to a time before the loss,"[6] nor can they imagine themselves ever again as part of a happy family of faith. Having trusted righteous religion so innocently, and having believed so completely, they no longer know who they can trust or what to believe. They had tried to be good and compliant children in order to stay in the good graces of the parental church. The intensity of their disillusionment, thus, parallels the intensity of love and attachment they once had for the parental church.

The grief over lost illusions does not last long because it is too emotionally, physically, and spiritually exhausting, and most people need to rest and heal "the scars of what is now missing in their lives."[7] What they thought was a good and solicitous parental church is no longer there, providing them with spiritual grounding, safety, support, acceptance, and community. In many ways, such believers have experienced a form of parental death and require a time of solitude and recuperation. This period of recovery offers them the opportunity to make peace with the past, soften feelings, reminisce about "the good times" in the Christian family, and move toward forgiveness. Because solitude and a certain distancing from the loss are essential for gaining perspective,[8] individuals need this time to pull back from the loss and reexamine it in a way that is less emotionally loaded.[9] It is from this vantage point that Catholics and Fundamentalists can obtain the objectivity necessary for the emergence of the real self.

THE STORY OF MARIA AND STEVE

Maria and Steve grew up together in a blue-collar neighborhood of a large city. Being next door neighbors since they were three years old, they were constant companions and considered each other much like a brother and a sister. Maria attended Catholic schools and Steve went to public schools, but each looked forward to watching TV, playing board games, and hide-and-seek after school, on weekends, and during vacation times. Even though Maria worshipped at St. Ursula's and Steve fellowshipped at Vineyard Bible, they didn't allow differences in religion to disturb their friendship. Steve's parents, however, were raised to believe that Catholics were not even Christian and that the Pope was the Anti-Christ. Similarly, Maria's parents taught her that Protestants would try to undermine her faith which Maria must protect as if it were a precious rose. Surprisingly, Steve and Maria were oblivious to their parents' prejudices, and eventually, the older generation softened and let the friendship flourish. Both sets of parents worked hard to provide their children with the basic necessities of life and a good foundation in Christian values. They believed that education was the primary vehicle for a better life and hoped that Steve and Maria would attend college. Fortunately, both were bright, helped each other in their studies, and won university scholarships after graduating from high school.

Maria

Maria was excited to be accepted at the nearby state university. Catholicism was a major part of her life as a freshman at the school and she was an active participant in Newman Center activities and at Sunday and even daily Mass. It was then her firm belief that the church would reward her goodness and loyalty by providing her safety and comfort. In her second year, she enrolled in a women's study course where her eyes were opened to the high rate of depression among women, their second class status in most cultures, and the relationship between the two. She began to read widely on the topic and learned of the patriarchy and its dominance in both organized religion and the social fabric of civilization. Gradually, her friendship network shifted from the Newman Center to the Women's Center.

One Sunday at Mass she looked up and noticed there were only men on the altar. She was surprised that this simple fact had never registered before. For the first time, she felt excluded from the faith that she always believed would include and accept her unconditionally. Over time she began to note the masculine and patriarchal tone of the Catholic environment. Men held the power over others and were referred to in terms such as Lord, Master, and King. Conversely, women were subservient to them and described by titles such as handmaidens and virgins. At one Mass, Maria lost count when the masculine references to both humans and God exceeded fifty. She suddenly felt like an outsider in her own Catholic home.

Looking beyond the local church, she saw how men made most of the decisions and presumed themselves to be all-knowing; in fact, women's voices were barely heeded in the writing of a pastoral letter on women. She had been raised with the understanding that as a loyal Catholic girl she would be listened to and communicated with by the priestly, parental generation. Her sense of disillusionment was deepened as she saw how seldom women were heard by the church fathers and with what inequality they were treated. Because of their gender, they were considered unworthy of the priesthood, yet were told how valuable they were in the eyes of the church.

Even after college graduation, she bargained with herself to remain an active member of her religion. In spite of her pain, there was a deep need to stay connected. She tried to convince herself that the church was imperfect since it was made up of flawed and frail human beings. She perceived that the weaknesses of the church reflected human fallibility rather than a deficiency in the gospel. She further reasoned that the excessive number of masculine references and hierarchical thinking recalled a time when Catholicism was forming. If there were to be any changes in this patriarchal structure, Holy Mother Church required a feminine presence. Should women like her abandon the faith, shifts in the ecclesial atmosphere would only be prolonged. Maria told friends, "This is *my* church and I'm not leaving; if anyone quits, it's going to be them!"

Some days, however, this stubborn defiance would turn into anger and she found herself railing against such church "fathers" as St. Paul and St. Augustine who had helped set this lamentable system into place. Such were her sentiments one Holy Family Sunday between Christmas and New Year's when she was in town attending Mass at St. Ursula's with her parents. When she heard the readings state that wives were to be submissive to their husbands, be like fruitful vines, and live in the recesses of the home, she knew she couldn't take it anymore. In deference to her parents, she remained through the service but vowed never to return.

For a period of time, it was a relief to be away from the church, but eventually she reached a point where she missed it. Maria experienced a surprising sadness as she remembered the happy times of family weddings and christenings. A profound pain would sometimes overcome her and the loss she felt was as intense as if someone close had died. She found herself preoccupied with her loss such that she had difficulty sleeping and would sometimes cry when discussing or even thinking about the church. It was almost as if nothing else mattered.

Maria began to spend more and more time alone. Although she maintained her friendships, much of her time was spent in solitude, trying to heal the wound. The pain eventually lessened and she felt more peaceful. Remembering the church didn't make her weep and she could recall the rituals, the distinctively Catholic sights and sounds, and the symbolism without feeling torn up inside. She intuited that a perspective was returning but she didn't know where it would take her.

Steve

Over the years, while both were attending college and beginning their careers, Maria and Steve talked on the phone and met for lunch whenever Maria returned to her home town. Steve couldn't understand what was so upsetting to Maria that would compel her to abandon her religion. After all, she had loved Jesus just as much as he when they were growing up and they had even helped each other with their religion projects. She had prepared him for his Bible quizzes, while he had helped her memorize over one hundred and fifty answers to the bishop's questions at Confirmation.

Being Maria's lifelong friend, Steve had tried to listen to her views but his years at the Calvary Bible Institute had made it difficult for him to be sympathetic. He reasoned that her attendance at the state university had caused her to lose her faith; conversely, his time at the bible college had only solidified his loyalty to religion. Steve was deeply concerned for his friend's spiritual well-being. On numerous occasions, he tried to talk some sense into her but all he got in return was what he considered radical feminist rhetoric. Try as he might, he couldn't comprehend the nature of Maria's distress.

Steve had worked hard for his degree in biblical counseling and had become an associate pastor at Vineyard Bible. He was proud to be called to the ministry of caregiving and was pleased when Pastor Dan Felton referred to Steve as "my prayer warrior." This affirmed the direction he had felt God intended for him when, at age thirteen, he had stepped forward at a crusade conducted by a famous evange-list and had accepted Jesus as his personal savior. This altar call at the local high school stadium had initiated his ministry of disci-pline, and being called a "prayer warrior" was like a blessing sent directly from God.

Steve gave witness to Christ in all aspects of his life. He took the headship of his household very seriously and loved his wife, Eve-lyn, as Christ loved the church. Together they trained their children in the ways of the Lord, keeping the Sabbath, and devoting time each day to sharing scripture. Steve enjoyed reading the Bible aloud to his children and paraphrasing it so that they could understand.

While Steve supported his family by selling life insurance, his heart was with the work at Vineyard Bible. He quickly established his position of leadership in adult Christian education. One of his first tasks was developing a prayer partnership group which he taught to respond to prayer requests, especially from people who were moved by God at the monthly altar call. His soldiers of the cross prayed with them in the power of Jesus' name to renounce the forces of wickedness often at work in their lives. Steve also orga-nized an evangelistic team who were led to minister on Skid Row. There he and his team devoted themselves to providing testimony for the Lord and to warning unbelievers of their impending damna-tion. They invited numerous individuals to come to Jesus and were successful in helping many to be saved.

Meanwhile, he attended the monthly staff meeting at Vineyard Bible, where the heads of the various ministries gathered to discuss their mutual concerns. As time went on, however, he grew increas-ingly unsettled by Pastor Dan's excessively controlling style of leadership. It was well known that Dan harbored ambitions to become the senior pastor of a large soul-winning congregation, as well as to establish himself as a televangelist with a large national following. In Steve's mind, this ambition accounted for his pastor's strong need to maintain order in his flock and a rigid adherence to gospel fundamentals so as not to jeopardize his chances of being called to greater things. The monthly meetings, therefore, were always well-orchestrated. Pastor Dan selected the agendas, determined what was allowable for discussion, manipulated the outcome of voting, and reserved to himself the right to make final decisions even on the slightest matters. Once the only item left for the staff to vote upon was whether to plant tulips rather than daffodils in the church's spring garden. Steve often left these meetings feeling that gospel values were being sacrificed to the pastor's ambitions.

There were other events that caused rifts in Steve's previously unquestioning faith. For example, rather than exemplifying Christ-like compassion for the poor on Skid Row, Pastor Dan often referred to them as "derelicts" and "sinners." Additionally, it became clear to Steve that the evangelistic outreach to the indigent was merely a tool for Pastor Dan to pull on the congregation's heartstrings and thus extract more sympathy contributions from them. But as Steve listened to the street people's stories he could no longer consider them simply as unsaved but, rather, as individuals struggling with difficult life circumstances. After working in the inner city for a year, he found that, in conscience, he could not continue to impose the burdensome message of impending damnation upon the already overwhelming burden of their impoverished lives. He saw that they needed a message of a loving and supportive God, rather than an angry, vengeful deity who further contributed to their despair.

Conducting biblical counseling and hearing the problems and dilemmas of church members also resulted in Steve seriously questioning some of his lifelong beliefs. He wondered whether some of his advice and freely offered biblical quotes were too simplistic to address the complexity of the problems he was seeing. He had believed that prayer would solve everything, but now he had his doubts. Steve also worried that his religion's harsh focus, judgementalism, and gloomy pessimism seemed to intensify rather than alleviate depression in many people. He had been taught to love the sinner but to hate the sin. He saw his notions of sin changing, however, as he met with people who were deeply in love with someone of their own gender, conscientious women who chose abortion rather than deliver a seriously deformed fetus, older people who opted to live together outside of marriage rather than forfeit their social security, and healthy young people who masturbated yet were terrified that this was leading them into demonic activity.

Listening to the struggles of the people led him to reassess the laws and practices of his religion. Whereas individuals came to him and to Vineyard Bible seeking the compassionate Jesus, they were instead taught about Christian warfare and doing battles with enemies. They came for something spiritual and for something to feed their souls, but were given worship whose quality was rated on its entertainment value. Verse-swapping and scriptural ping-pong seemed to Steve to act as substitutes for understanding the real word of God. Likewise, Steve could no longer uphold his religion's belief that humans were basically evil and "the saved" needed to separate themselves from the lost. He couldn't agree with the notion that God was angry at these "unclean wretches of humanity" (as Pastor Dan called street people), and that a loving God would come to punish sinners while saving the righteous who had simply accepted Jesus as their personal savior. Steve was beginning to see that religion was more than individual salvation and that true believers should not segregate themselves from struggling people whom they deemed sinners but, rather, should work among them as Jesus did.

These concerns were on his mind when Steve convened the monthly evangelistic team meeting. When the discussion centered on strategies on how to save souls on Skid Row, he found the righteous tone of the conversation quite troubling. He took that occasion to express some of his doubts concerning the way the team was approaching the individuals to whom they ministered. He told them how troubled he was about the amount of legalism and judgmentalism at Vineyard Bible. By the time he finished, he had disclosed the range of his concerns about the nature of God, salvation, sin, and biblical inerrancy.

Word of his remarks quickly reached Pastor Dan who scheduled an appointment with Steve for the next day. Knowing that the pastor was a reasonable and godly man, Steve felt assured, upon entering the meeting, that the two of them would enjoy a prayerful and productive discussion about Steve's concerns. Without so much as a call to prayer, Pastor Dan admonished his former prayer warrior for not upholding Christian standards. Dan informed Steve that in order to retain his leadership position, he needed to repent of his doctrinal errors and publicly recant his views before the evangelistic team.

Pastor Dan's preemptory admonition stunned Steve. He deeply desired to share his concerns with this man who he considered to be a mentor and Christ-like leader. However, each time Steve brought up a specific topic for discussion, Dan interrupted him, telling Steve that any further dialogue would only waste their time. The pastor quoted 1 Timothy 5:20, "Those who sin are to be rebuked publicly, so that the others may take warning."[10] Thus, Steve was given no other choice but to repent before the evangelistic team. Failure to do so, Pastor Dan informed him, would necessitate a public censure and eventual disfellowshipping. Steve attempted to bargain with Dan but this proved futile. Without so much as a closing prayer, Dan walked out of the meeting leaving the secretary to escort Steve out.

Steve refused to conform to the pastor's demands. In a tersely worded letter, he informed Dan of his decision. The following Sunday, in front of the whole congregation, the pastor censored Steve for his refusal to repent and asked the church members to treat the former leader as they would "a pagan or a tax collector" (Matthew 18:17).[11] According to the pastor, Steve had committed the unforgivable sin, that of impenitence, and thus was now disfellowshipped at Vineyard Bible.

While Steve fought against his feelings of anger and sadness, he vowed that he would not let this get him down. With surprising speed he enrolled himself and his family at the local United Methodist Church which he understood had an outreach program to the poor. He immediately volunteered to help this ministry in its work with the homeless. Soon, Steve felt included in his new church community and frequently let his former Vineyard Bible friends know how happy he was at United Methodist. He often retold the story of the bitter treatment he had received from Pastor Dan. Somehow, he felt compelled to replay the negativity of that experience, probably in an effort to convince himself that he hadn't lost much by his departure.

Gradually, however, his denial weakened as he recognized how much he missed certain aspects of his religious heritage. While Vineyard Bible and United Methodist had some things in common, he was poignantly aware that he was an outsider. Many of the hymns were different, the sermons often lacked the solid biblical grounding he once enjoyed, and there was little of the familiarity and fellowshipping style he had been raised with at Vineyard Bible. Additionally, United Methodist was wary of his biblical counseling degree and wouldn't allow him to hold leadership positions in the church. Over time, Steve came to understand Maria's sense of religious alienation and marginalization.

None of the ways that Steve had once used to keep his spirits up seemed to work. He was always an energetic individual who would throw himself into church or business projects rather than sit and think about his troubles. Now he was preoccupied with the circumstances that led to his estrangement. Up until his confrontation with Pastor Dan, he looked to the church as a model for fair play and justice. He had assumed, as in a business relationship, that if he did his share, the church would do likewise. He felt disillusioned, devalued, and uncared for by a parent-like institution that had promised to stand by him until the end. These feelings boiled inside of him and he finally had to share them with someone. Fortunately, Maria was in town visiting and he went over to visit her. With few words exchanged, they hugged each other and cried.

Steve had never let himself feel this deeply before. The men in his family had been conditioned not to cry and their task was to comfort the women. He had always felt it was his job to console Maria but now it seemed as though the roles were reversed. His natural tendency was to flee painful feelings and his friend had to continually remind him that he needed to feel his sadness in order to resolve his loss. By spending hours alone for the first time in his life, he was learning to comfort and soothe himself.

MOVING TOWARD THE REAL SELF

The story of Steve and Maria illustrates what many Fundamentalists and Catholics experience when confronting their illusions regarding the parental church. Both had tried to be good and compliant children and had loyally adhered to the teachings and practices of their churches. In turn, they unconsciously expected religion to protect and guide them, keeping their very best interest at heart. It was almost as though a bond of trust existed between them and the church.

That bond was broken for Maria when she saw that her very being was somehow second class in the eyes of the church fathers. While women were often extolled in extravagant terms, the other side of the message was that there was something "lesser than" or unequal about them when it came to decision making or liturgical practice. Like Steve, she did not feel heard or communicated with and both experienced a deep sense of injustice. In this regard, Steve trusted that the church would treat him equitably and not resort to self-righteous and judgmental methods in its dealings with him. He was proud to be a prayer warrior at Vineyard Bible and was indebted to his religion for preaching about fairness and equality. What he discovered, however, was that the very church that had taught him about the good and compassionate Jesus was conducting its business in a punitive, exclusionary, and dictatorial manner.

Both Maria and Steve experienced a violation of their trust, which compelled them to examine religion more critically. When confronted for the first time by the falsehoods imbedded in many of their religious beliefs and expectations, their first inclination was to protect themselves from the pain of disillusionment. Maria engaged in a lengthy bargaining process with her church, trying to give both herself and her religion every benefit of the doubt. The thought of breaking her relationship with the church was unbearable. Steve, on the other hand, took the offensive by attempting to discuss differences with Pastor Dan in an effort to hold on to his illusions. When it became apparent that he wouldn't be heard and that repenting was his only option, Steve saw more clearly the reality that the illusions masked.

Both Maria and Steve took the most time-honored avenue for letting go of Catholicism and Fundamentalism; they left. Steve sought to minimize his loss by immediately becoming an active participant in another denomination. Maria couldn't face another patriarchy and so remained separated from organized religion. Like her friend, however, Maria tried to devalue the importance of Catholicism in her life by belittling, discrediting, and ridiculing the religion at every opportunity.

Gradually, the full dimension of the loss became apparent to them. All their efforts to ward off the intense sense of betrayal by their religions proved futile and both, in his and her own way, felt the extent of their loss of faith. Once they allowed themselves to experience these true feelings, a strange sense of peace emerged, probably because they were no longer expending effort fending off undesirable emotions. Maria and Steve then entered a grace-filled time when, in solitude, they learned to comfort themselves and allow perspective to return. They were no longer fleeing the pain of disillusionment, but were more emotionally and spiritually available for the real self to unfold.

In Chapter 1, ten capacities of the real self were discussed. Steve and Maria's progress through disillusionment succeeded in peeling off the masklike persona of the compliant child or false self. This unmasking, then, revealed more and more of their own voices or true selves. Steve and Maria's journey to the real self is best captured by six of Masterson's ten capacities.[12] (Chapter 18 will deal with these as well as with the remaining four capacities.) Although this passage to self and spiritual transformation is a life-long endeavor, the two friends began the process in the following ways:

- *The capacity to experience a wide range of feelings deeply:* Relinquishing the role of the good and compliant Christian, neither Steve nor Maria felt a need to edit their feelings during the most emotionally intense period of their crises of faith. Shorn of illusions and feeling invalidated by the parental institution, the friends lacked the defenses to censor the raw emotions of the real self.
- *The capacity to expect entitlements:* As has been discussed previously, authoritarian religion often usurps basic rights and many believers grow up not feeling entitled to the same rights for due process that they have as citizens of society at large. They may not feel entitled to make their emotional and spiritual needs known in the church or to seek redress for grievances from the institution. Steve and Maria, however, realized they deserved more responsive parenting and spiritual mentoring than they received.
- *The capacity for self-activation and assertion:* The church does not countenance assertion or self-direction in its faithful

but rather encourages acquiescence and passivity. Maria and Steve took a strong stand on their own behalf after a lifetime of conditioning to submit their wills to the authority of righteous religion. This initial movement toward the true self will be expanded in Chapter 18 when both Maria and Steve will take a public step in the interest of their own integrity.

- *The acknowledgment of self-esteem:* Unlike many obedient Christians, neither of the childhood friends asked themselves what they had done wrong to precipitate their departure from the church. Having somehow escaped the tendency of self-blame so characteristic of many Fundamentalists and Catholics, Maria and Steve instinctively realized that the deficiencies resided within the church and not within themselves. Having been taught that they were created in the image of God, they saw that the issue wasn't their worthiness but, rather, the illusions inherent within righteous religions.

- *The ability to soothe painful feelings:* By not having access to the teachings and practices of their religion during this time of trouble, Steve and Maria could not rely on the church for guidance and comfort. Thus, in this period of disillusionment and uncertainty, they came to realize that God could exist apart from religion. Further, they experienced the Divine as an internal source of comfort, who abided with them as they learned to hold, soothe, and comfort themselves.

- *The ability to be alone:* The threat of exclusion constantly hangs over the heads of Catholics and Fundamentalists, and Steve and Maria were not immune to this fear of abandonment. By entering into solitude and spending time alone, they both discovered that their worst fears were unfounded. Rather than greater disorientation, they encountered the peace necessary for the unfolding of the real self.

CONCLUSION

It is a truism that if people live long enough most of their illusions will shatter. Religious illusions are no exception. In fact, living in any relationship for a lifetime—whether it be with a person, family, a country, or a religion—requires coming to grips with disillusionment. Only those individuals who conduct their lives mindlessly and blind to reality, or set in rigid beliefs, escape having to deal with the uncertainty brought about by religious disenchantment. For the rest of the population, when illusions begin to deconstruct and disillusionment with a primary relationship occurs (in this case with the parental church), a loss process is initiated. In this chapter, the passage through grief has been conceptualized as a peeling away of the false self to allow a gradual emergence of the real self.

The first step, then, for people who are disillusioned with righteous religions is to reframe that experience as normal and potentially growth-enhancing, rather than as a tragic situation occasioned by their own weakness, sinfulness, or neglect. Grieving pains are often growing pangs if individuals allow them to be recast in such a manner. What may seem so much like dying and destruction can be viewed as a birthing experience.[13] In fact, the upset and turmoil at this stage are symptoms not of illness but of religious transformation, reflecting "a deep psychological shift from identification with the defensive self to the actualization of the real self."[14]

The task for spiritual pilgrims, then, is to stay with their emotions, rather than foreclose on a process rich with potential for psychological and spiritual growth. The temptation often is to avoid, minimize, or sidestep the pain and turmoil in a number of ways. Some people refuse to see any problems with their religion and may be offended by what they consider disloyalty in those who do question their faith. When illusions start to shatter, others shift into a problem-solving mode and try to fix the situation. Some cut themselves off from religion altogether and may refer to themselves as "Ex-Catholics" or "Recovering Fundamentalists"; others join another religion far too quickly before they have allowed themselves the opportunity to grieve their lost heritage. A substantial number simply stay angry with righteous religion for the rest of their lives, yet remain in the church.

Thus, rather than denying, bargaining, or cutting off from their religion, individuals are invited to stay with their emotions, letting them assist the real self in emerging. At the same time, *Righteous Religion* is written to provide the perspective necessary for readers to view their disillusionment more from a distance and less totally from the vantage point of their loss. In a sense then, experiencing emotions while concurrently having an objectivity about these emotions are not contradictions, but rather essential elements of an ongoing and healing process. As with any growth trajectory, both "staying with" and "stepping back" work hand in hand to effect movement toward the real self.

"Rather than every religious illusion dying of disenchantment as a person's mind matures, one's religious beliefs undergo continuous transformation and revision, simultaneous with other developmental progress."[15] Thus, the crumbling of illusions can be viewed as a step along the path toward spiritual transformation. The next phase of growth involves learning to live comfortably with the paradox and ambiguities inherent in religious faith.

Chapter 18

Living with Paradox

David Steindl-Rast makes the point that many Catholics, who are deeply bonded to the church, live in a system of double-messages that he terms a "spiritual schizophrenia."[1] As earlier chapters of this book have demonstrated, righteous religion, on the one hand, purports to be a provider, protector, and guide; while on the other, reveals itself as a conditional parent operating within an inconsistent and contradictory system. Pythia Peay comments on Catholicism and the work of Joseph Campbell as follows:

> To be born a Catholic is to inherit a spiritual conundrum. Those deeply affected by the tradition can spend a lifetime attempting to harmonize the opposites of spirit and matter, inner truth and outer authority, even love and hate for the Church itself. Catholicism beckons the soul with its treasure house of mysteries, its daily feast of the wisdom of saints, the poetry of mystics, the prophetic utterances of seers. At the same time, with its dogmatic insistence on correct moral and political behavior, it repels the sensibilities of a contemporary person.[2]

Maturing Fundamentalists, likewise, sense the contradiction between the deepest spiritual realities of their faith and the personal and political practices of churches. Many yearn for the feast that Christianity can provide, yet, desiring bread, they are instead fed stony rules, prohibitions, doctrines, and the letter of the law. The expectation for spiritual awakening pitted against the receiving of authoritarian demands for compliance sets the stage for the paradoxes experienced by many members of authoritarian religions.

As *Righteous Religion* has discussed up to this point, maturing Catholics and Fundamentalists often experience ambivalence. When the contradictions become apparent between their idea of core gospel values and the actual ways authoritarian religion implements them, believers often feel disillusioned and betrayed. Theologian Richard McBrien provides a list of principles, values, or moral imperatives that he believes are at the heart and center of the Christian gospel and with which Fundamentalists and Catholics would undoubtedly concur:[3]

- the call to love one another;
- the call to love even our enemies;
- the call to forgive one another;
- the call always to seek reconciliation with one another;
- the call to renounce revenge;
- the call to avoid judging and condemning others;
- the call to avoid self-righteousness, presumption, and resentment toward others;
- the call to befriend those whom society looks down upon;
- the call to serve one another, humbly and unselfishly;
- the call to serve the poor;
- the corresponding call to beware of riches and the attachment to possessions; and
- the call always to be just in our dealings with others.

These imperatives of Jesus Christ permeate the gospels and have been instilled in Catholics and Fundamentalists from childhood. Bible-believers can quote Matthew, Mark, Luke, and John, chapter and verse, citing proof of their soundness and validity. Many Catholics can tell stories of saints who exemplified each of these values. As believers from both traditions become conscious of the illusions at work within their churches, they observe how consistently authoritarian religion contradicts its most cherished principles. Instead of love, forgiveness, and justice, maturing Christians see institutions that undermine the inherent goodness of individuals, often judging, discrediting, excluding, and scapegoating members. Rather than befriending and serving society's outcasts, Christians are witnessing whole groups being shamed and alienated from the pulpit. In place of a clergy which serves humbly, they behold a leadership that offends their sense of justice, while often lording over their congregations in a superior or self-righteous manner. Desiring a haven of reconciliation and honest dealing, believers perceive how righteous religion stifles the voices of members, thwarts spiritual maturity, and closes rather than opens channels of communication.

As good and compliant children, Catholics and Fundamentalists frequently have not allowed themselves to acknowledge these inconsistencies. Being faithful Christians, they have been conditioned to consider any negative sentiments toward their churches as being the handiwork of Satan and the seeds of rebelliousness against God. In this regard, they have often been reminded that their religion is good and they are bad (i.e., sinful and unredeemed). Furthermore, having "bad" emotions, such as doubts about righteous religion, additionally underscores their dire need for salvation.

As discussed in the previous chapter, individuals need to trust that within these apparent dichotomies reside the elements necessary for spiritual integration and reformulation. They also need to believe they can grow in objectivity and perspective about their religion by staying with these discordant inconsistencies and the accompanying emotions. The process of living with righteous religion's polarizations and contradictions is frequently disturbing to the conscience, however. A certain tension exists which is recognized as an incompleteness. A compelling need for some action often arises from this tension that will begin the process of healing the breach between themselves and what is essential in their religions. In this regard, people come to sense that it is time to move beyond disillusionment and breached trust and learn to live with the paradoxes that have been part of their spiritual life.

Maturing believers, at this stage, experience a renewed courage to risk and a willingness to be vulnerable again to religious experience. Having relinquished the hope of being back in their religion in the same way as before, they are now nevertheless committed to doing what it takes to restore and integrate some new form of spirituality. They are mustering the courage to weave together a religious expression authentic to themselves, fashioned from beliefs retrieved from their faith heritage, newly-acquired insights, and the guidance of inner wisdom.

While the steps needed for integration are occurring, signs of a more congruent spiritual life and a renewed hope in a loving and present creator begin to emerge. Left behind are the easy assurances, familiarity, and predictability that were the most identifiable rewards for complying with the parental demands of a righteous religion. But what lies ahead for believers is a vague yet compelling sense that they have begun to move closer to spiritual integration and that somehow God is a vital player in their unfolding transformation.

However, simply knowing all this is not enough to allow people to live comfortably with religion's paradoxes or to reframe a previous view of their churches. Maturing Christians must take some appropriate public step to integrate lost illusions and ambivalent feelings about Catholicism and Fundamentalism. For individuals to resolve their issues with righteous religion, an active step that is harmonious with their emerging true self is essential.[4] Believers may now see their religion from a more honest perspective, but ask how that knowledge will help them move on. There still remains a tension that requires combining action with awareness. Growing individuals, having come to a "painfully acquired knowledge of self,"[5] now realize that their relationship with the church is unfinished and begs for resolution.

Given the diversity of emerging Catholics and Fundamentalists, public steps of integration are equally diverse. Some will feel the need to do something which integrates a fresh sense of self within the context of their religion, while others are compelled to leave entirely the arena of righteous religion in order to consolidate the fragments of their spiritual beings. Regardless of the paths chosen, examples of such public steps might include:

- writing a letter to a religious leader, such as Pat Robertson or the Pope;
- making a donation to a religious charity which addresses the needs of society's marginalized or outcast individuals;
- revisiting a childhood church;
- attending a church supper with their mothers;
- starting a support group for people like themselves;
- talking to grandparents about their religious heritage;
- reading a book about spirituality;

- listening to tapes about world religions;
- conducting a ritual and saying good-bye to the church;
- selecting psalms from the Bible that speak of a loving and comforting God;
- choosing a spiritual director who is independent of their tradition;
- sending their judgmental pastor a birthday card;
- devoting an hour on Sunday to taking a walk and speaking to God in nature;
- sitting at the bedside of someone who is dying;
- compiling a list of the gifts they received from their religion;
- joining a dream group where the spiritual content of dreams is explored; and
- forgiving themselves for not forgiving the church.

The possibilities are endless and frequently reflect both the creativity of maturing Christians, as well as their newfound willingness to take risks and act courageously. They intuit that, until they act upon what they know, nothing will change and the yawning sense of incompleteness will continue. By taking an active step toward pulling the pieces of their religious lives back together again, they are well on their way toward spiritual cohesion and wholeness.

John Schneider, who writes about the transformation of loss, contends that "to integrate a loss, we need to believe that the important aspects of what we lost won't be forgotten and will remain a part of us."[6] In other words, people can't turn their backs on their losses and then expect that they can be whole again. Schneider believes that they must remember their losses and remind themselves of what they have *not* lost in order to restore the integrity of their souls. It is through this restoring and remembering, then, that people remove the obstacles that stand in the way of cooperating with God in recreating their faith.

Once a public step of remembering, restoring, and recreating has been undertaken, there is a sense of freedom and renewed hope. This self-activating movement constitutes a genuine self-expression that reflects growing maturity. It is an event in which the bad or compliant child would never have engaged. People are now in a place where they can see themselves and their church through a new set of eyes. The wisdom of the real self, the voice within, rather than external authority, is directing their actions. The action of a public step—the first of many—unblocks energy, creating shifts both internally and in perspective.[7]

Once trapped spiritual energy is released, believers feel more open to allowing their faith to unfold. The intensity of the search for the perfect faith is diminished as what previously seemed fundamental is altered. Rather than seeking just the right answers, they realize that many possible ways to express their faith exist. As a result, new possibilities emerge and there is a relinquishing of many of the old practices, teachings, authoritarian demands, and reliance on external reassurances. With this increased flexibility and openness, individuals somehow realize that these had to be surrendered in order to move into deeper spiritual connections. They now understand that even the pain of disillusionment was necessary to reformulate the images of faith.

In this vein, Catholics and Fundamentalists often feel, perhaps for the first time in their lives, that they are unconditionally good in the eyes of God. With this more complete sense of loveability they are more open to, and accepting of, themselves and others. Maturing Christians, thus, begin to trust intuition and the wisdom of their bodies rather than relying on the guidance of righteous religion. In other words, they are starting to reframe themselves, their religion, and the nature of spirituality.

Additionally, previously disillusioned believers now experience a diminishing of dichotomies and a greater balancing of polarities. Rather than nursing righteous indignation about the inconsistencies of religion, they find themselves better able to appreciate the numerous paradoxes inherent in Catholicism and Fundamentalism. They discover a capacity to tolerate ambivalence and to live with their feelings of both love and hate toward their religion. These contradicting emotions are always present in any relationship where there is intense love and attachment; the experience of individuals who are bonded with their faith is no exception. People who are members of righteous religion often have extreme splits between good and evil or dichotomizations between the saved and unsaved, and will continue to do so until there is an integration of these seemingly opposite and irreconcilable polarities. John McDargh, a psychologist of religion, summarizes well what is probably the most life-altering insight of this new awareness: "It is trust that endures the realization that most objects of my attachment are at their best less than my idealizations would have them and at their worst better than my severe judgments upon them."[8]

Once the illusions about righteous religions are thus reformulated, the church is no longer expected to be a perfect and eternal parent, a mental health clinic, or a completely functional family system. Rather, growing Fundamentalists and Catholics are trusting in the capacities of the real self by learning to take care of themselves, be alone, soothe their painful feelings, and in general supply their own parenting. Through these processes, they are able to find their own voice of spiritual truth.

THE STORY OF MARIA AND STEVE: CONTINUED

Maria

With the passage of time, Maria's career in public relations flourished. She was able to purchase a home and enjoyed entertaining friends there. On the surface her life was successful; but inside, she felt incomplete, as if something vital were missing. Maria knew it had to do with her Catholic tradition and the lack of resolution in her spiritual life. She was so disillusioned by organized religion that she didn't even bother to seek another church or religious community.

At the prompting of her friends, Maria decided to join them for a weekend retreat at a Catholic convent that rented its facilities to outside groups. She sensed that this might be an ideal opportunity to finally say good-bye to the Catholic Church. So she mustered her courage, paid her registration fee, and drove with her companions to the rural retreat center. When she arrived on Friday night, Maria felt turned off by the fervor of some of the participants but nonetheless she resolved to attend Saturday morning Mass as a farewell gesture. As she sat in the back of the chapel the next day, she was surprised when a peacefulness washed over her. The priest felt comforting and seemed to make a conscious effort to include references to women throughout the service. The singing of the nuns, the familiarity of the Mass, and the faint aroma of incense in the air elicited memories of her childhood days at St. Ursula's. The entire experience caused her to remember how she had loved the church so much back then. Maria also began to understand why she had never been able to leave Catholicism comfortably.

At breakfast that day, an elderly nun sat down in the chair beside her. Soon, they were talking about the service that morning and Maria found herself telling Sister Barbara her story. As they conversed, Maria discovered that they had many similar experiences with Catholicism. Both had been disillusioned by the injustices and inconsistencies they had seen, and both had felt invalidated in the same ways. Maria was moved when Barbara told how at one time she had contemplated leaving religious life, but like Maria, something had continued to call her back.

When Maria found out that Sister Barbara served as a spiritual director at the retreat center, she didn't hesitate to ask if she could make bi-weekly appointments. They agreed that the purpose of these meetings would be to explore the significance of Catholicism in Maria's life, reconcile the paradoxes that were confounding her, and integrate her tradition as she reformulated her faith. The knowledge that she was again being vulnerable to a self-righteous religion frightened Maria, but somehow, she felt that a loving God must have placed Barbara in her life for some reason.

Over the succeeding months, Maria found that she was in a personal process of restoring and recreating essential parts of herself and her faith. She and Sister Barbara discussed many matters, particularly Maria's guilt at being a disloyal Catholic. In this regard, Maria needed to validate her own intuitive wisdom and to absolve herself of the arrogance implied in assuming that her wisdom was equal to that of the church. Sister Barbara listened carefully and affirmed the courage of Maria's choices as well as her attempts at restoring her own integrity. Maria felt free to express the depth of her anger at Catholicism and with the nun's help, was able to acknowledge her inability to forgive the church's violations of the human spirit. This declaration was forgiving in and of itself.

An important result of her meetings with Sister Barbara was that

Maria knew she needed to take some concrete steps to activate her insights. She realized that she wanted in some way to recreate the religious rituals that meant so much to her. Likewise, she yearned for a community with whom she could celebrate the integration of her old faith with her new spirituality. By placing announcements on the retreat center's bulletin boards, she was able to gather a group of individuals with whom to explore various religious expressions.

The success of the group lay in its ability to help members express their spirituality honestly and openly. Each week, different people led the group in a manner that was religiously meaningful to them. The gatherings often included music, ritual, sacred readings, sharing, and meditation. As a result of her involvement with this community, as well as her continued sessions with Sister Barbara, Maria was more balanced and integrated and saw fewer dichotomies between Catholic traditions and her new religious expressions. She felt entitled to trust her own voice, intuition, and spiritual creativity. In this new wisdom, Maria felt a greater oneness with God and yet, along with her joy, there existed a sadness at having lost an innocence about her once-beloved church.

Steve

Eventually, Steve wandered away from the Methodist church. He sought out other churches but felt equally alienated and unsettled in each. Even though they all employed scripture and preached Jesus Christ, they seemed to exhibit the same sense of judgment and self-righteousness that he had experienced at Vineyard Bible. Once his church-shopping had run its course, Steve was at a crossroads. Either he could continue selling insurance and remain bitter and resentful toward righteous religion; or he could follow his call from Jesus and pursue a graduate degree in counseling at a nearby university. Steve's heart was still with the poor and outcast, but his biblical counseling degree didn't qualify him for the necessary licensure to work in a mental health field. After discussing this with his wife, Evelyn, they decided that she would support him on her teacher's salary while he went to school. This important step of following his inner spirit took all the courage he could summon, but Steve knew he had to do it to restore his own integrity.

Part of his educational program required Steve to seek therapy, and he did so at the University Counseling Center. Through this and his course work, he realized he had to tie up loose ends with Pastor Dan and achieve some closure on his unhappy experience at Vineyard Bible. After considerable thought and prayer, Steve decided to draft a letter forgiving his former paster for his treatment. After all, Pastor Dan was only doing what St. Paul had instructed. Also, Steve was coming to realize that, had it not been for the events surrounding the disfellowshipping, he wouldn't have felt free to create a new and more authentic form of ministry for himself. With these thoughts in mind, he was able to complete and dispatch a letter with a true sense of forgiveness in his heart.

After considerable work, Steve earned his counseling degree. He had completed his internship at a United Way mental health agency that served low income clients. The supervisor liked his work so much that after Steve finished the hours required for licensure, the director offered him a full-time job. Many of the people who were now coming to him for help were individuals he had met earlier when he was on the evangelization team for Vineyard Bible. Having been marginalized by his own church, he could now more readily relate to their alienation. This identification increased empathy such that he was able to reframe his work as a renewed form of ministry. Further, Steve came to feel that he had been placed in this setting to do God's work and to give witness to Jesus.

In the course of his employment, Steve heard many people speak favorably of a mission down the street. There, he was told, gospel values were preached and everyone left feeling loved and affirmed. Steve was surprised to hear clients who had once renounced all churches for being hypocritical and self-serving now singing the praises of Good Shepherd Rescue Mission. He learned that the pastor was formerly a homeless alcoholic who had given his life and will to the care of Jesus. Steve was determined to meet this man who so exemplified the loving Savior; he walked down the street and introduced himself.

Steve and Pastor Elias hit it off immediately. Over the succeeding months, the two visited often, discovering they had many similar experiences with righteous religions. Both had been active in bible-based churches and had been disfellowshipped–Steve for speaking out and Elias for abusing alcohol. Steve began worshipping regularly at Good Shepherd Mission and the pastor encouraged Steve to select for group singing his favorite hymns from his days at Vineyard Bible. Soon, Steve was conducting the noon Bible Study classes where he deliberately focused on passages that reflected the loving and compassionate God that both he and Pastor Elias had come to know.

Steve also felt called to pray at the bedsides of those who had no one to sit with them as they died. During his times of prayer, Steve felt fully confirmed in his service to God's people. This was the ministry he had been searching for at Vineyard Bible but was unable to find. His new way of living and preaching the Gospel felt authentic and liberating, compared to the judgmental and often unloving tone of his former religion. While he was still angry at the injustices perpetrated by authoritarian religions in the name of a loving Lord, Steve was simultaneously able to see the goodness of the message proclaimed by these churches. Surprisingly, his anger was increasingly tempered by his affection for his religion. Likewise, he discovered this newfound ability to both love and disdain the church to be freeing.

Steve invited Maria to join him and other volunteers in serving the Thanksgiving meal at the mission. The next day they took some time to reminisce about the recent events of their lives. Maria recounted her meeting Sister Barbara and the formation of the spirituality group. In the course of the discussion, they realized their paths, although divergent, had brought them to essentially the same juncture. Both agreed that they now felt closer to God and more spiritually alive than ever before. The issues that troubled them about their religions didn't bother them anymore. There was still pain as they recalled St. Ursula's and Vineyard Bible, but there was also joy as they remembered some of their childhood religious experiences. Furthermore, they both expressed a sense of peace and comfort at having integrated some of these more special traditions into their current spiritual practices. Steve and Maria felt that God was speaking to them in an intimate way and guiding them as they created a unique blend of both the old and the new in their lives. They now felt free to create new opportunities and religious meanings as they revised old beliefs and formed new ones.

FROM INCOMPLETENESS TO INTEGRATION

In the midst of their pain and disillusionment with Catholicism and Fundamentalism, Maria and Steve attempted to cut themselves off from their religions. While this tactic worked for a time, a sense of incompleteness and irresolution hampered them from moving on in their spiritual growth. Both Maria and Steve discovered they needed to make peace with the past and reclaim and integrate those elements of belief that continued to be life-giving.

Once they allowed the authority of dogmatic religion to crumble, they began to challenge many of their former religious practices and moral prescriptions. By thus stepping outside of the framework and systems of righteous religions, they started to view the world through their own frame of reference. They saw their religions from new perspectives and thus were able to give new interpretations to their religious experiences.[9] As Dana Crowley Jack contends, such individuals become actors and authors of their own stories and "not the subject of someone else's plot."[10]

The closer Maria and Steve came to being "authors of their own plots," the closer they were to their own authentic voices and real selves. In this regard, Masterson's attributes of the real self (discussed in Chapters 1 and 17) again describe their experience. Having become architects of their own religious lives, they continued to believe they had the right to have their spiritual needs met. Further, Maria and Steve asserted a personal integrity that allowed them to create their own religious visions and narratives in an active and self-reliant manner. Four additional Masterson attributes apply at this stage of growth:

- *The ability to make and stick to commitments:* They followed the promptings of the Holy Spirit in composing and substantiating their personal and spiritual integrity.
- *Creativity:* Maria and Steve refashioned old, and familiar religious traditions, interweaving these with fresh and personally authentic ones.
- *Intimacy:* They expressed themselves fully and honestly to a religious mentor and, in the process, came to trust in the wisdom of spiritual companions.

- *Continuity of self:* Having grieved the loss of illusions and religious structures, Steve and Maria appreciated deeply the abiding presence of God and a personal core that is eternal.

CONCLUSION

Human beings are by nature relational and communal and thus the passage to their inner, eternal core usually takes place in the company of others. This was true for Steve and Maria, both of whom gravitated toward individuals who were able to provide a source of mutual support and mentoring. The two friends missed bring a part of something bigger than themselves and felt cut adrift in their religious lives. Sensing they could not heal in isolation,[11] they intuitively sought out spiritual companions with whom they could express their fears, doubts, insights, hopes, and visions.

Through these connections, Steve and Maria experienced new possibilities for relatedness and came to see that it was possible to integrate their rituals and traditions with their new voices of faith. Thus, the nature of their relationship with religion shifted. They were able to tolerate the simultaneous existence of paradoxes such as love and hate, acceptance and rejection, and attraction and revulsion with the parental church. They arrived at this reconciliation "by a trusting loyalty to the Principle of Being (which) enables a kind of whole-seeing that moves the individual beyond lesser allegiances and conflicting commitments and towards a vision of the whole as God might see it."[12]

What believers like Maria and Steve come to develop and integrate in their faith lives is a "whole-seeing," or an ability to view the bigger picture as seen through the eyes of God. They begin to incorporate those values and principles, mentioned earlier, that reside at the heart of the Christian gospel into a broader panorama of the human and the divine. Just as maturing people are able to tolerate and balance contradictory emotions toward their parents or their country, this can be done with their churches as well. They are no longer as tightly bound to the "lesser allegiances and conflicting commitments" of righteous religions, but are able to reject the hypocritical and destructive aspects of such institutions while simultaneously embracing what is life-giving from their rituals and messages.

The judgmental, unloving, and self-righteous aspects of dogmatic religions that were once at the foreground of their thinking fade into the background once believers take a public step of integration. With this movement comes a shift in focus that allows the values and principles of the Christian gospel to move to the center of their consciousness. Rather than being caught up in bitterness or incompleteness, they are more free to concentrate on loving others, reconciliation, forgiveness, compassion, social justice, and oneness with God.

By remembering, restoring, and recreating, Catholics and Fundamentalists are able to integrate the most vital and transformative elements of their religions. Since humans don't cut off any aspect of their past without cutting off a part of themselves, their traditions must at least be revisited. With this journey backward into time can come an extraction of those elements that have sustained both their personal and religious families for generations. Part of this process will inevitably involve a recognition and ultimately a resolution of the numerous religious paradoxes and contradictions encountered along the way. The reward to be gained by Catholics and Fundamentalists who courageously undertake this pilgrimage, however, is the discovery of their own spiritual voice and a renewed hope.

Chapter 19

Transforming Illusions

Religion serves an essential human purpose and plays an important role in lifelong development. As previous chapters have demonstrated, righteous religion can contribute to disillusionment and
distress, but by the same token, the truths inherent in authoritarian
systems also provide vital avenues for transformation. Once individuals have taken steps to integrate life-giving traditions with new
spiritual insights, their relationship with religion begins to change.
With this shift, there is "a new reclaiming and reworking of one's
past" as well as "an opening to the voices of one's deeper self."[1]
Believers are now "alive to paradox"[2] and aware of the truths
contained in what had previously seemed contradictory. A clarity of
vision, a "whole-seeing," emerges which allows them to see
beyond injustices into a core of eternal, universal truth. Maturing
Catholics and Fundamentalists have begun to make peace with the
fact that truth can be viewed from a number of perspectives. With
this objectivity, such Christians can choose to be a part of their
congregations without being consumed by them. Likewise, some
may elect alternative spiritual paths.

Up to this point, *Righteous Religion* has dealt largely with what is
occurring in individuals' external lives. It now concludes with an
exploration of maturing believers' inner spiritual world. These
people have undergone changes in their relationships with religion
in that they no longer view it through the distorting lens of illusions.
They see righteous religion for what it is and whatever ties exist are
more authentic. Having addressed one of their most important and
intimate relationships, they have a greater capacity for more authentic connections in other areas, namely with the core of their beings.
Because they are closer to their souls, (their real selves), maturing

Christians can be more intimate with God. They are now able to serve as their own parents, to affirm, hold, and comfort themselves, and hence, can accept a God who acts in a similar manner. The following section will explore both the nature of that close and personal relationship with the Divine, as well as the origins of human imagery for God. With this understanding, individuals will be able to identify those conditions that are essential to their religious transformation. Since authentic spiritual experience involves feeling safe, affirmed, and befriended, people will be able to recreate these same experiences as they develop personal forms of religious symbolism, prayer, and ritual.

GOD

For many, the origins of their imagery for God is derived from the parental relationship. The effects of the early emotional environment, the way parents imprint themselves on offspring, and the nature of that interactive process are fixed so deeply in the psyche that they are inextricably and unconsciously interwoven with imagery of God. People often feel around God the way they felt when they were diapered, cared for, and talked to as infants. The presence, moods, rhythms, feelings, gestures, and environment offered by parents and the way infants perceive them is eventually translated into an image of God.[3] While there is not a "simple correlation between parental images and God images,"[4] there is sufficient support for the notion that people's concepts of God are constructed from, and are fairly consistent with, early experiences of their parents.[5] "The . . . representation of God is an imaginative creation or active construction of the developing child, conditioned by . . . the characteristics of the parents."[6]

The premise underlying this section is that for religious experience to be viable, it must in some way replicate a good parenting relationship. As previous chapters have demonstrated, Catholicism and Fundamentalism have often served as conditional parents by accentuating imagery for God that is judgmental, critical, and punitive, rather than affirming and comforting. Because maturing believers have developed the capacity to discover the real self, they are now able act as their own parents and create the internal conditions that allow for the acceptance of a God who reflects their worth. In other words, they no longer gravitate toward a harsh and alienating God but rather are drawn toward a God who mirrors their true and gracious beings. This beckoning God provides safety, reflects goodness, and continually abides with them.

The God of Safety

In times of stress, most people feel an acute need to be held and comforted. For many, this need is fulfilled by an image of God carrying or rocking them much as their parents did when they were infants.[7] It is believed that individuals have a "somatic memory"[8] of such parental comforting that lays down a foundation for the experiences they expect to find with God. If infants experience their early environment as safe and benevolent, they often have the essential "psychic raw material" for a later representation of God as likewise safe and benevolent.[9]

The sense of safety and trust (or lack thereof) in infancy sets the stage for a subsequent encounter with a protective or nonprotective providence.[10] Consider the situation in which most infants are immersed. They are entirely dependent on another, seemingly omnipotent being, who surrounds them and sustains their life. This "hallowed presence"[11] of parents lays the foundation for future representations of a God, who similarly is as faithful, shielding, all-powerful, and trustworthy throughout their lives. Humans seek to replicate the rhythms, moods, patterns, and affective tone of this early "holding environment."[12] Efforts to reproduce the tone of this maternal ambiance compel people to seek a parallel sheltering presence with a divine protector.

The writers of scripture capture reminiscences of this shielding environment by conveying images of a benevolent and comforting God. As the father of compassion, the "God of all comfort" comforts children in all their troubles (2 Corinthians 1:3-4). In fact, God's unfailing love is the source of all comfort (Psalms 119:76). The Creator is portrayed as a mother who will never forget her children (Isaiah 49:15), who will nurse them at her comforting breasts, and who will dandle them on her knees (Isaiah 66:11-13). The God of the psalmists is one who enables children to sleep in peace and dwell in safety (Psalms 4:8).[13]

The words of the psalmist are carried into the Catholic rite of baptism with God being invoked as a refuge under whose wings the newly baptized may take shelter (Psalms 61:3-4).[14] In the same rite, God is described as a shepherd providing the flock with refreshment, repose, and safety (Psalms 23).[15] A Eucharistic prayer of the church reflects the protective theme of the shepherd when God is pictured as one who never leaves the flock untended and who watches over and guards it always.[16]

If children grow up without a sense of "being somehow at one with a benevolent and provident reality,"[17] they later may lack the ability to experience a God who is described as comforting, nurturing, consoling, or shepherding. When the circumstances of the early holding environment are lacking and the needs of infants are relegated to the needs, whims, and wishes of the primary caretaker, future representations of God may very well be characterized by inconsistency, capriciousness, and a general lack of dependability. This inability to trust undermines "the enduring belief in the attainability of fervent wishes,"[18] and thus damages individuals' potential for hope. With the absence of hope and a history of unfulfilled needs, prayer seems futile, salvation unpredictable, God fickle, and the universe unsafe and precarious. Righteous religion often capitalizes on the fears and insecurities of such individuals and recreates a familiar parental environment.

The God of Goodness

The foundation for humans' ability to see themselves and God as good (or bad) is laid down in early infancy by a process known as mirroring. In their exchanges with parents, infants see themselves reflected in their caretakers' faces and, accordingly, develop feelings about themselves. It is in the mirroring process that children come to know themselves "as good in the reflected appraisal of the parent"[19] and, thus, are affirmed in their loveability and uniqueness. For example, mirroring occurs when babies are fed, changed, called by name, talked to, bathed, greeted, and burped. The quality of these interactions, the eye contact, and the parent reflecting the infant's emotional states, are all essential ingredients for establishing a child's sense of self and well-being. Positive mirroring is a matching process whereby parents "perceive the unique characteristics of the child's emerging self" and respond "to these in a positive, supportive manner."[20]

For children who have been well-parented, the mirroring function of "recognizing eyes and reconfirming smiles"[21] is extended to God who sees the child as good and lovable in much the same way as the parents do. This early experience of being reflected in a mother's reaction resides at the core of an infant's God representation.[22] So important is this relationship that it influences the infant's future "affective bond with the sacred." In fact, one's relationship with God may be seen as an enacting or reenacting of the primary parental relationship that helped to constitute the self.[23] These patterns of relatedness[24] are carried through a lifetime, are established during the rhythms and tones of early infancy, and are extended to all relationships, both human and divine.

Babies looking into the faces of their mothers or fathers gain a sense of being known, of seeing themselves reflected in the parental gaze. Pre-images of God have their origins in these exchanges, in which "the rudimentary awareness of self as separate from and dependent upon the immensely powerful others"[25] is formed. If the parental "mirror is cracked or darkened, our sense of self will be distorted,"[26] as will be the image of God. In other words, images and elaborations of God are colored by the early mirroring experiences, whether positive or negative, with the primary caretaker.[27]

Scripture presents God as a positive mirroring caretaker in the first chapter of Genesis wherein humans are described as being created in the image of God and being looked upon as "very good" (Genesis 1:27, 31).[28] That God is a loving mirror is expressed in the Catholic liturgy of Trinity Sunday when the church asks God to "be near to the people formed in your image, close to the world your love brings to life."[29] Like parents looking warmly at an infant, God, in one of scripture's most ancient blessings, is called upon to "make his face shine upon you . . ." and "turn his face toward you and give you peace" (Numbers 6:25-26).[30] Psalms, playing on the theme of the face of God, testify that the Creator's kind visage instills a sense of contentment and safety upon those whom God gazes (Psalms 31:16; 17:15; 80:3, 7, 19).[31]

In addition to being looked upon kindly, individuals wish to be known. As parents gazing on their children convey a sense of knowing them, so also God sees the faces of the children and knows them (1 Corinthians 13:12).[32] Similarly, children desire to see God and "with unveiled faces all reflect the Lord's glory" (2 Corinthians 3:18).[33] Believers are encouraged by scripture "to gaze on the beauty of the Lord" (Psalms 27:4) and to "seek his face always" (Psalms 105:4).[34] The theme of the just, the childlike, and the holy seeing the face of God and being mirrored therein is a popular one in scripture (Psalm s11:7; Matthew 18:10).[35] It is perhaps best recognized in the negative, where the psalmist uses the theme of God hiding (his) face to illustrate the feelings of being forgotten, disempowered, rejected, terrified, dismayed, repelled, and cast into darkness (Psalms 10:11; 13:1; 27:9; 30:7; 44:24; 88:14; 104:29; 143:7).[36] So deep is the need for positive parental mirroring that without this loving reflection people feel intense distress. Not only is their sense of self distorted but so also is their image of God. Maturing believers, having developed the capacity for positive mirroring, now find the rejecting God imagery of righteous religion discordant with their emerging spirituality.

The God of Abiding Presence

The ability to hold an image of an unseen God emerges in the first seven or eight months of infants' lives. Prior to this developmental milestone, children believe that people and objects are extensions of themselves. The paternal hand and the maternal breast are theirs and do not exist separate from themselves. As infants mature, they begin to realize that objects and others have an independent life of their own. At one time "out of sight" was "out of mind"; now a longing for the misplaced person or thing prevails. Nature comes to the rescue, however, and allows for the ability to construct and retain mental images of these absent people and objects.[37]

This phenomenon of "object permanence" allows children to remember what is not present. If this so-called "object" is a mother, the memory of her when she is absent can sustain the little ones and help them still feel connected to her. Thus, infants virtually take their parents inside of themselves, swallow them whole, and incorporate them into their personalities. Humans literally become one with their parents and carry the history of the parent/child relationship within themselves. This internalized parental presence casts a long shadow that travels with people throughout their lives.[38]

It is in infancy that humans begin the process of seeking out objects that carry with them the "assurance of well-being which was reflected in early life by the actual presence of the parents."[39] Objects such as a favorite blanket or doll evoke a sense of security in children and enable them to negotiate life's more difficult transitions. Thus, they are called "transitional objects." In order to manage the business of separation, children invest these items with a private significance that allows them to feel safe while the parents are away. Hence, transitional objects have "a remarkable capacity to soothe and comfort the child in moments of anxiety."[40]

Transitional objects assume symbolic qualities that are often very different from the characteristics of the items themselves. It is not so much the teddy bear itself, but what the teddy bear represents and how the child feels toward and with the teddy bear that is important. Being with the stuffed toy evokes for children rhythms of the earliest and most comforting experiences with their parents.[41] The memories of these interpersonal relationship patterns and "the emotional tenor of early interactions" become transitional objects themselves and provide the grounding necessary to feel safe and cared for in life.[42] Feeling protected, individuals are freer to tackle other transitions, to work, play, create, and go about the business of living.

God enters the picture by serving the same function as other transitional objects. God keeps individuals safe in the world and quietly offers "the silent reassurance of an almost imperceptible presence."[43] Children begin to form representations of God based on their experiences with their parents and later from relationships with their siblings, family members, and "the general religious, social and intellectual background of the household."[44] The need to develop some form of concrete object representation for God arises from youngsters' quest to navigate through childhood's traumas and fears toward a sense of self that is both separate from their parents yet somehow securely related.[45] This passage involves projecting onto God good parental objects. Thus, God as internalized parent may function as the "all accepting Other" who, like a "good-enough" mother, acts as the "guarantor and preserver of the background of safety"[46] that allows for play, creativity, and the emergence of a sense of self. Such God representations, derived from parental images of trust and mutuality, make it possible to love unconditionally, accept life's ambiguities, and be alone with the Alone.[47]

God eventually may function as the One who is present with the growing child, replacing to some extent the parents who are seen as fallible and limited. This transitional God, the one many humans carry with them throughout their lives, provides a perpetual holding and comforting environment as well as the experience of being mirrored by a benevolent and ultimately accepting parent. Such images help to recreate the cadences and emotional tones of the early caretaking relationships when parents were consistently dependable, loving, and available.[48] Such experiences imprint themselves on human memory as something positive, growth enhancing, and capable of transforming one's being. For many, God is sought after and surrendered to as the "over-powering, awe-inspiring, compelling, and inexhaustible" agent that promises the metamorphosis of a person's internal emotional world.[49]

What happens when the cadences and emotional tones of the early holding environment are perceived as rejecting, unresponsive, or abandoning? These, just like their more positive counterparts, are imprinted within the impressionable memories of children and become an integral part of their personalities. Since at this stage parents and children are one, children of "conditional" parents automatically take the "badness" of the relationship into themselves. These little ones are helpless and intuit that they need good protective caretakers for their survival. They must do everything they can to make the world safe, even if it means blaming themselves "for all the pain being experienced so that the outside world can remain guiltless and good."[50] Somehow there is more security in seeing themselves as bad, guilty, and sinful rather than living in an evil or unsafe world.[51] This coping phenomenon has been described earlier as the good/bad split.

Since God images are based primarily on parental images, one of the only ways for self-perceived sinful people to negotiate the traumas and fears of life is to see themselves as bad, and their parents, and by extension God, as good. Additionally, the only way "bad" people with good/bad splits know how to please a "good" yet potentially rejecting, unresponsive, or abandoning God is to conform to a nearly endless list of divine prohibitions and to do nothing that might jeopardize the tenuous relationship with this abiding presence. Righteous religion provides a home for self-perceived sinful people and offers them a means to placate this rebuffing and forbidding deity.

At the core of this paradox is fear of abandonment, carried over from the early holding period and projected upon virtually all relationships including the one with God. Having internalized the rejection of their parents, they see themselves as potentially discardable and no amount of compliance, conformity, prayers, or repentance can eliminate the "badness" or burden of evil they so deeply feel. Thus, the long shadow of the critical and judgmental parent/God abides with them until such a time as their sense of self becomes stronger and more reflective of an empathic and sustaining deity.[52] Maturing Christians find themselves at this juncture in their lives.

Scripture and church rituals give ample witness to a God of abiding presence, but the images are as diverse as the memories and projections that emanate from early human experiences. Representations of God range from a consistently loving presence to an angry, rejecting avenger wrecking havoc not only on enemies, but also on faithless and traitorous children. God is seen in scripture and liturgy as the good shepherd who never leaves the flock untended and whose love will remain constant no matter what trial or distress occurs (Psalms 23, John 10:1-18, Romans 8:35-39).[53] Should God's children pass through the waters, God will be with them; should they walk through fire, they will not suffer (Isaiah 43:1-2).[54] The Lord's overarching presence casts a long shadow and is seen in the images of protective lodging, sheltering wings, (Psalms 61:4), and cooling shade (Psalms 121:5-6).[55] To make concrete these images of safety and to carry with them the abiding protection of an unseen God, Christians employ a variety of transitional objects, such as crosses, Bibles, stained glass windows, incense, hymns, statues, pictures of Christ, and even the sights and smells of old churches.

People with ambivalent parental imprinting may identify with and gravitate toward scriptural, catechetical, and liturgical references to a seemingly contradictory God, who is described not only as good but also as vengeful and angry. For example, the prophet Nahum speaks of the Lord as good, "a refuge in times of trouble" (Nahum 1:7) and, almost in the same breath, as "a jealous and avenging God" (Nahum 1:2) who "will not leave the guilty unpunished" (Nahum 1:3).[56] The *Catechism of the Catholic Church*, which is asserted to be "a sure and authentic reference text for teaching catholic doctrine," describes God as faithful, compassionate, merciful, gracious, trustworthy, constant, truthful, and infinitely good. At the same time, however, God is said to have "fierce anger" and, as with the angels after their fall, will not permit repentance for sin after death.[57] A common response to this ambivalence is found frequently in the Mass, where the faithful take the "badness" onto themselves, project all goodness onto their caretaker God, and petition repeatedly for forgiveness and deliverance. Assuming the posture of unworthiness, they proclaim to God that "we are nothing without you," tell the Lord that "I am not worthy to receive you," and ask God not to give "what we truly deserve."[58] Exposing the fear of parental abandonment underlying the good-God/bad-self dichotomy, the liturgy has the priest, immediately before receiving communion, praying "never let me be parted from you" and "let it [the communion] not bring me condemnation."[59]

RECAPTURING THE SACRED

The relationship between the early environments of infancy and the later imaging of God has been the focus of this section. Rather than desiring to return to the womb, humans more accurately seek to replicate the real or imagined atmosphere of infancy, calling forth its rhythms, tones, and maternal ambiance. Many find this ambiance in the sheltering providence and the loving gaze of God. Some, having internalized an unresponsive, ostracizing, or somehow tenuous presence, project similar imagery onto God. Still others, unable to feel safe with a rejecting parent or God, will assimilate the badness onto themselves, investing all goodness into an all good but potentially forsaking Other.

Catholicism and Fundamentalism, perhaps inadvertently, often replicate earlier, unsafe environments for people who hold negative images of God. These individuals find themselves at home in righteous religion because the total milieu and parenting style feels familiar. Maturing believers, who are now mirroring an affirming and accepting deity, are no longer comfortable in such surroundings because the God proclaimed there is so discordant with their current internalization of the divine. They know that God exists for them when they feel safe, when their inherent goodness is reflected back to them, and when they feel the Creator closely residing with them.

Transforming Christians seek to experience inwardly and manifest outwardly these essential features of their relationship with God. The remainder of this chapter will illustrate how these core elements of safety, goodness, and abiding presence can be recaptured in prayer, religious symbolism, and ritual.

Prayer

Prayer serves believers in their quest for oneness with God. As people mature in faith, their definition and manner of prayer changes. Previously, when they were under the influence of righteous religion, their prayers were often addressed to a judgmental and critical God and conveyed a placating, apologetic, and self-deprecating tone. Since this God's love appeared conditional, believers often asked to be saved from the consequences of their actions. Prayers frequently reflected fear and guilt and focused almost exclusively on begging and pleading for salvation and acceptance. God was over and above them and they were lowly, unworthy creatures trying to win *His* favor. Prayer forms, which were pre-set and dictated by their religion, offered Catholics and Fundamentalists only childlike formulas for communicating with a distant, parental God.

When believers change, so also do images of God and, hence, their ways of relating to that God. They are no longer children badgering a reluctant Deity for their needs but, rather, adults capable of intimate contact with themselves and with God. Because the parent God now resides within them, believers are capable of immersing themselves in experiences of prayer that are more direct and personal. They now pray to a God who reflects their most inner and private belief systems and prayer becomes "a channel for expressing what is most unique, profound, and personal in individual psychology."[60] This is a dramatic change from their days of apologizing for their emotions and begging forgiveness for the yearnings of their souls. Since God is an intimate part of their beings, prayer has become a mutual conversation between lovers.

Authoritarian religion offers believers only a limited image of God and translates faith into a rigid set of rules and responsibilities intended to please this rigorous, salvation-dealing deity. Theologian Ana Marie Rizzuto believes, however, that as people go through life and bring new experiences to their inner representational worlds, their God-image is reworked to reflect the new conception of self. In other words, Christians can outgrow a brittle or rigid image of God if they allow their concept of God to shift as they evolve. With this transformation, the relationship between the two of them can be life-giving, hopeful, and reciprocal.[61] Thus, God and believers can assume a conversation that is direct and without the mediation of authority figures who presume to speak for the distant deity. People can now approach God directly in prayer because, as they have evolved, they have become one with God.

During prayer, believers surrender to God; in the process, God becomes a "medium that alters the self."[62] Just as in a relationship between lovers, the act of giving oneself to the beloved other produces a change in the giver. This self-donation is such a powerful process that a spiritual metamorphosis occurs and people are forever changed. The key to this transformation is the depth of trust that individuals invest in this newfound loving God. Whereas previously this trust had been mediated through righteous religion, it is now placed in a God who is inseparable from themselves.

Prayer, then, is an ultimate act of love, the surrender or giving of self into the accepting hands of the divine. It brings individuals full circle, back to the times when, as infants, they abandoned themselves peacefully into the arms of loving parents. This letting go without fear reflects the willingness of believers to assume a child-like posture of trust in and reliance upon an unconditionally loving God, who abides through them, with them, and in them. Thus, the internalization of this divine presence permits praying Christians to be alone because they are never truly alone. Prayer then emanates from believers' developing capacity to be at one with their real self.

No longer are they entering into righteous religion's dark harbor of fears and doubts but, rather, emerging into the place where they and God are forever one.[63] Such an experience of God "support[s] the emergence of the True Self and mediate[s] the faith that makes it possible to tolerate dependence, accept ambivalence, embrace aloneness and love unreservedly."[64]

Religious Symbolism

Christians who are developing a more intimate understanding of God want to translate it into symbols that are harmonious with this emerging relationship. Symbols or sacred objects often enhance the art of prayer since both are capable of effecting an inner ambiance of reverence that accompanies oneness with God. In their selection of sacred symbols, maturing believers must learn to trust in their own intuition and remind themselves that they now have enough experience and perspective to choose from the old traditions as well as to incorporate new ones. In a sense, they now have the courage to do what Catholicism and Fundamentalism condemn–shop around for viable expressions of their image of God. Like Dorothy who went to Oz, maturing believers now realize that God is what they deeply sense God is, even though righteous religion tried to tell them otherwise.

Much of authoritarian Christianity has demanded that believers view symbols only from the church's viewpoint and that any other perspective was heretical, misleading, or blasphemous. For example, such key symbols as Christ, the crucifixion, heaven, hell, the virgin birth, and resurrection were to be seen only as concrete and historical people, places, and events rather than representations capable of evoking resonances on deeper emotional levels. As individuals mature spiritually, they become capable of moving beyond the literal and often fixed interpretations prescribed by righteous religion. Not only is paradox appreciated, but reality can be seen from a number of perspectives. Key elements of religion are viewed not only on a concrete level but also on numerous symbolic levels. People, then, are now capable of entering into rich dwellings of religious meanings and symbols, and into what is termed the mystical level of reality. For example, the crucifixion is not simply an historical event that occurred 2000 years ago but also a daily experi-

ence of the Divine participating in the many crucifixions and sorrows of individuals' lives.[65] As theologian W. W. Meissner points
out, "the crucifix is not just a piece of carved wood, nor is the Torah
simply a roll of parchment with ancient writing on it. Rather, they
are religious symbols and as such become the vehicles for the
expression of meanings and values that transcend their physical
characteristics."[66]

These sacred objects, according to Meissner, stand on the boundary between the internal and the external, the subjective and the
objective. In other words, individuals attribute their own personal
and private meanings to religious symbols since they evoke a different set of experiences in each person and are influenced by all levels
of the mind and spirit. Maturing believers having transcended the
constraints of righteous religion, can allow their own multidimen-
sional forms of spiritual expression to emerge and take form.

Each symbol designated as sacred will inspire, as in prayer, a
sense of reverence as well as evoke an earlier time of enchantment
and magic. When in the presence of a personal sacred object, people
feel safe and embraced by an ever-present and loving creator.
Believers feel a sense of oneness, "an uncanny fusion,"[67] a welling
up of hope and confidence, recalling an ambiance reminiscent of
infancy where they once felt embraced, soothed, comforted, and
protected by a Godlike parent. These religious symbols or events
have the capacity to transform maturing Christians by returning
them to an earlier state of total union with a beloved. These conscious and unconscious reminiscences create shifts on such deep
levels that "powerful metamorphoses of being"[68] result and a significant altering of self occurs.

Concrete objects, such as crosses or Bibles, possesses the capacity to propel individuals into prayerful states or transitional realms;
sensory experiences such as sounds, smells, and sights do so as
well. Rather than reverencing only those objects that righteous
religion deems sacred, maturing believers are free to choose from a
whole panoply of symbols that bring the experience of God to life
in the here and now. For example, some people find the sound of a
choir alters their internal landscape; others find this sense of transformation in sunsets, the hands of their grandmothers, a poem, an

opera, a magical painting, the laughter of children, the aroma of incense, or the sun radiating through a chapel window.

Rituals

Rituals, like symbols, assist individuals in capturing an earlier, sacred atmosphere, making the reality of God alive in the present moment. Rituals help to bridge the unconscious world to an experience in the outer world. The more such an experience is familiar, the more capable it is in evoking a sense of the transcendent.[69] Historically, some forms of ritual have helped individuals, particularly children, absorb the myths, manners, customs, and mores of their social group. By participating in these cultural rites, people are socialized to become competent and functioning members of their social order.[70] Rituals such as the use of table manners, Christmas gift giving or opening, or the proper way to address adults relate people to the familiar, giving them a sense of societal grounding. Other rituals help celebrate life transitions. In this regard, baptisms, marriages, funerals, and retirement parties provide continuity from one life state to another.

All rituals engage people in a story of how life proceeds. These sagas emanate from the cultural past and offer a foreshadowing of future direction, thus endowing individuals with a blueprint for their lives. This map also serves a grounding function which affords predictability and safety. For example, a birthday party is a ritual representing a milestone in the passage from birth to death, a marker that the person is progressing along the life/death trajectory and a communal sign of love and support on that journey. Myths are shaping stories that "render in contemporary terms the mysteries of our own inner life, and the relationship of these mysteries to the cosmic life."[71] Religious rituals are particularly adept at reenacting these myths because they translate a vision of God into ritual activity. By participating in religious ceremonies, believers participate in the myth.

Joseph Campbell contends that there are common themes or elementary ideas "that occur in all the mythologies and all the religions of the world." For Christians, these motifs of good and evil, death and resurrection, and surrender and transcendence are represented in Christ's crucifixion. In this signal event, believers are invited to give themselves to "the grace of a transpersonal realization." The cross, then, becomes the symbolic "threshold of the passage of eternity into time and of time into eternity," illustrating the mythological theme that those who lose their life shall find it.[72] Before scriptures were written or codified, Christian communities acted out the legends and sagas of their faith, employing story and song to bring it alive in the context of their life struggles. Thus, the role of religious liturgy was to add to tradition, evoke meaning from myth, inspire commitment, and encourage all members to carry on.[73]

Life-giving rituals enhance the rhythmic poetry of the written word so that the power of God's compelling message can be heard at the deepest levels of the self. These rituals speak to the core of the being, at the level of unaddressed and unconscious assumptions that shape beliefs. The heart, as well as the mind, is moved.[74] Vibrant rituals focus participants both inside and outside themselves toward a transcendent, whole-seeing God. In other words, effective Christian ceremonies reenact the reality of an interior abiding and comforting God as well as one who elevates and inspires the imagination. Additionally, rituals embody symbolisms expressing connections with the past and offer passages into a hope-filled future.

Unfortunately, not all rituals prove to be life-giving or vibrant. Rather than instilling hope in participants, some rites "become magical talismans in the service of magical expectations and infantile needs." With these "obsessional rituals, . . . religious faith is corrupted into ideology."[75] This certainly is the case with much of righteous religion's approach to worship, wherein both Fundamentalist scriptural interpretations and Catholic liturgical practice are adhered to in a literal, rigoristic manner. Authoritarian religion tends to offer rituals that are concrete rather than abstract, literal rather than symbolic, stereotyped rather than creative, repetitive rather than spontaneous, rational rather than mystical, and cognitive rather than affective.

As people grow in their faith, ritual emerges as "heightened interest in the symbolic aspects or explanations of God" and such individuals find they can no longer respond to the "deadening ritualism" of dogmatic religion.[76] Maturing Christians do not need to be told what their symbols mean and are "beyond" rituals used for indoctrination and rites that define what righteous religion wants them to believe. Rather than ceremonies that reduce their symbols and images to words, growing Catholics and Fundamentalists desire rites that are like works of art in that they speak for themselves through the eyes and the senses to the listening heart. Instead of repetitive prayers, theological summations, words and more words, they appreciate a balance between words and images that "render insights beyond speech."[77]

Theologian James Fowler, in describing stages of faith, affirms that mature believers can appreciate ritual because they have grasped the extent of reality to which they refer. Such individuals are capable of assimilating "new depths of experience in spirituality and religious revelation." In other words, by opening to the voice of the "deeper self," believers are able to create rituals that further enliven and enhance the capacities of the real self.[78]

Thus maturing Fundamentalists and Catholics, knowing that they need not rely exclusively on the rites and ceremonies of their respective traditions, are fashioning rituals that are more expressive of the Spirit's voice within. For example, Miriam Winter contends that rituals can be used to celebrate three rituals: creation, liberation, and transformation.[79]

- *Creation rituals* honor God's generative hand in all the universe. They solemnize occasions of new birth and sanctify the works of creation both human and divine. In this sense, the elements of earth, air, fire, and water as well as flowers, music, choreography, and art help develop the theme and ambiance in ritual ceremonies.
- *Liberation rituals* also use primal elements like fire and water as well as poetry, candles, greenery, and other materials to facilitate the passage through life. Scripture in particular is called upon as a source of wisdom in sacred seasons such as Advent, Christmas, Lent, Easter, and Pentecost.
- *Transformation rituals* observe important life transitions such as retirement, marriage, coming out, divorce, illness, death, recovery, and relocation. Like other rituals, these generally occur in a community wherein the movement from death to life and loss to transformation is eased and assisted.

CONCLUSION

The passage from death to resurrection is the central theme of Christianity. Through the process of unmasking their religious illusions, maturing believers have come to appreciate the personal relevance of Christ's message. Having dismantled some of the false assumptions regarding their faith, they have struggled to give birth to their true selves and personal voices of truth. In a sense, then, a rebirth has occurred. Rather than simply protesting the old, they have learned to look both backward and forward, both reclaiming the best in the traditions and transcending that which is no longer viable.[80] They feel alive and hopeful as they embark on a creative, imaginative, and mystical spiritual journey.

Reference Notes

Introduction

1. Catholic Biblical Association of America, *New American Bible* (New York: Catholic Book Publishing Company, 1970), 33.
2. Ibid.

PART ONE: ILLUSIONS ABOUT RIGHTEOUS RELIGION

Chapter 1: Toward an Authentic Voice

1. Erik M. Erikson, *Identity and the Life Cycle* (New York: W. W. Norton, 1959); James W. Fowler, *Stages of Faith: The Psychology of Human Development and the Quest for Meaning* (San Francisco: Harper and Row, 1981); W. W. Meissner, *Psychoanalysis and Religious Experiences* (New Haven: Yale University Press, 1984); Moshe Halevi Spero, *Religious Objects as Psychological Structures: A Critical Integration of Object Relations Theory, Psychotherapy, and Judaism* (Chicago: The University of Chicago Press, 1992), 64-65, 66-69.
2. Kathleen Y. Ritter and Craig W. O'Neill, "Moving Through Loss: The Spiritual Journey of Gay Men and Lesbian Women," *Journal of Counseling and Development* (Vol. 68, No. 1, 1989), 9-15. [Reprinted in Mary Thomas Burke and Judith G. Miranti, eds., *Counseling: The Spiritual Dimension* (Alexandria, VA: American Counseling Association, 1995), 127-141.]
3. Dana Crowley Jack, *Silencing the Self: Women and Depression* (Cambridge, MA: Harvard University Press, 1991), 32.
4. Ibid., 168-169.
5. Ibid., 33.
6. Ibid., 32-33, 37, 158.

7. James F. Masterson, *The Real Self* (New York: Brunner/ Mazel, 1985), 40; James F. Masterson, *The Search for the Real Self* (New York: The Free Press, 1988), 61.

8. James W. Jones, *Contemporary Psychoanalysis and Religion: Transference and Transcendence* (New Haven, CT: Yale University Press, 1991), 89.

9. Ibid.

10. Masterson, *The Search for the Real Self,* 42-46.

11. Ibid., 44.

12. Ibid., 45.

13. Jones, *Contemporary Psychoanalysis and Religion,* 103-107.

14. Fowler, *Stages of Faith,* 184-198.

15. L. Patrick Carroll and Katherine Marie Dyckman, *Chaos or Creation: Spirituality in Mid-Life* (New York: Paulist Press, 1986), 46.

Chapter 2: Religion as the Fortress of Absolute Truth

1. William L. Kelly, *Women Before God,* 3rd ed. (Westminster, MD: The Newman Press, 1961), 40.

2. William A. Carroll, ed., *Catholic Girls Manual and Sunday Missal* (New York: Catholic Book Publishing Company, 1952), 491.

3. Ibid., 31.

4. Ibid., 25.

5. Kelly, *Women Before God,* 39.

6. Carroll, *Catholic Girls Manual,* 54.

7. Austin Flannery, gen. ed., *Vatican Council II: The Conciliar and Post Conciliar Documents,* "Lumen Gentium" (Collegeville, MN: Liturgical Press, 1975), 395.

8. National Conference of Catholic Bishops, *The Sacramentary* (The Roman Missal Revised) (New York: Catholic Book Publishing Company, 1974), 209.

9. Pope John Paul II, *Catechism of the Catholic Church* (New York: Image Doubleday, 1995), 279.

10. Robert I. Bradley and Eugene Kevane, *The Roman Catechism* (Boston, MA: St. Paul Editions, 1985), 278.

11. Vatican Congregation for the Doctrine of the Faith, *Instruction on the Ecclesial Vocation of the Theologian,* May 24, 1990. Full text reprinted in the *National Catholic Reporter,* July 13, 1990 (Vol. 26, #35), paragraph 19.

12. New York International Bible Society, *The Holy Bible, New International Version* (Grand Rapids, MI: Zondervan Bible Publishers, 1983), 1105.

13. Ibid., 739.

14. Ibid., 1041.

15. Ibid., 1110.

16. Ibid., 1084.

17. Ibid., 1063.

18. Ibid., 1083.

19. Ibid.

20. Ibid., 1085.

21. Ibid., 1054.

22. Ibid., 1105.

23. Ibid., 963.

24. Ibid., 1051.

Chapter 3: Religion as a Parent

1. New York International Bible Society, *The Holy Bible, New International Version* (Grand Rapids, MI: Zondervan Bible Publishers, 1983), 1057.

2. Robert I. Bradley, and Eugene Kevane, *The Roman Catechism* (Boston, MA: St. Paul Editions, 1985), 108.

3. Pope John Paul II, *Catechism of the Catholic Church* (New York: Image Doubleday, 1995), 247.

4. Austin Flannery, gen ed., *Vatican Council II: The Conciliar and Post Conciliar Documents*, "Lumen Gentium" (Collegeville, MN: Liturgical Press, 1975), 421.

5. New York International Bible Society, *The Holy Bible*, 1120.

6. Ibid., 1031.

7. Flannery, *Vatican Council II*, "Lumen Gentium," 353.

8. Ibid., 383.

9. New York International Bible Society, *The Holy Bible*, 984.

10. Ibid., 1086.

11. Ibid., 1061; 1062-1063.

12. Ibid., 1095.

13. Flannery, *Vatican Council II*, "Lumen Gentium," 358.

14. New York International Bible Society, *The Holy Bible*, 697.

15. Ibid., 681, 1068, 1071.

16. Ibid., 1052.

17. Ibid., 1128.

18. Flannery, *Vatican Council II*, "Gravissimum Educationis," 729-730.

19. New York International Bible Society, *The Holy Bible*, 1096.

20. Ibid., 1102.

21. Ibid., 1092, 1113.

22. Ibid., 910.

23. Pope John Paul II, *Catechism of the Catholic Church*, 256.

24. Bradley and Kevane, *The Roman Catechism*, 359.

25. Bennett Kelly, *Saint Joseph Baltimore Catechism*, rev. ed., (New York: Catholic Book Publishing Company, 1969), 124-126; Patricia Klein, Evelyn Bence, Jane Campbell, Laura Pearson, and David Wimbish, *Growing Up Born Again* (Old Tappan, NJ: Fleming H. Revell, 1987), 51-88.

26. Kelly, *Saint Joseph Baltimore Catechism*, 125.

27. Ibid., 1091.

28. Ibid., 1132.

29. Ibid., 925.

30. Ibid., 64-65.

Chapter 4: Six Illusions of Religion as the Good Parent

1. New York International Bible Society, *The Holy Bible, New International Version* (Grand Rapids, MI: Zondervan Bible Publishers, 1983), 168.

2. Ibid., 920.

3. Ibid.

4. Ibid., 1098.

5. Ibid.

6. Ibid.

7. Ken Abraham, *Stand Up and Fight Back* (Ann Arbor, MI: Servant Publications, 1993), 35.

8. J. I. Packer, *Concise Theology: A Guide to Historic Christian Beliefs* (Wheaton, IL: Tyndale House Publishers, 1993), 261-263.

9. Ibid.

10. Ibid., 263.

11. Michael Francis Pennock, *This is Our Faith*, (Notre Dame, IN: Ava Maria Press, 1989) 237.

12. Ibid.

13. Robert I. Bradley and Eugene Kevane, *The Roman Catechism* (Boston, MA: St. Paul Editions, 1985), 479.

14. New York International Bible Society, *The Holy Bible*, 920, 1122.

15. Ibid., 906, 987, 1020.

16. Abraham, *Stand Up and Fight Back*, 170.

17. Pennock, *This Is Our Faith*, 234.

18. Abraham, *Stand Up and Fight Back*, 64.

19. The International Commission on English in the Liturgy, *The Rites of the Catholic Church* (New York: Pueblo, 1983), 986.

20. Ibid., 984.

21. Pope John Paul II, *Catechism of the Catholic Church* New York: Image Doubleday, 1995), 11; Bradley and Kevane, *The Roman Catechism*, 102-103.

22. Ibid., 537.

23. "Doomed: Baptists Say 46.1% of Alabamans Going to Hell," *The Bakersfield Californian* (September 19, 1993), A8.

24. New York International Bible Society, *The Holy Bible*, 1057-1058.

25. Ibid., 1045-46.

26. Ibid., 992.

27. Ibid., 5.

28. Ibid., 1128.

29. Abraham, *Stand Up and Fight Back*, 55.

30. New York International Bible Society, *The Holy Bible*, 404; Abraham, *Stand Up and Fight Back*, 32.

31. New York International Bible Society, *The Holy Bible*, 1448.

32. New York International Bible Society, *The Holy Bible*, 1041, 1085, 1045.

33. Ibid., 1096.

34. Ibid., 1098.

35. Ibid., 168.

36. Ibid., 642.

37. Pope John Paul II, *Catechism of the Catholic Church*, 294.

38. Bradley and Kevane, *The Roman Catechism*, 553.

39. National Conference of Catholic Bishops, *The Sacramentary* (The Roman Missal Revised) (New York: Catholic Book Publishing Company, 1974), 563.

40. Packer, *Concise Theology*, 165.

41. Patricia Klein, Evelyn Bence, Jane Campbell, Laura Pearson, and David Wimbish, *Growing Up Born Again* (Old Tappan, NJ: Fleming H. Revell, 1987), 142.

42. New York International Bible Society, *The Holy Bible*, 1042.

43. Ibid., 1046.

44. Ibid., 1113.

45. Ibid., 897.

46. Ibid. 1076.

47. Bennett Kelly, *Saint Joseph Baltimore Catechism*, rev. ed. (New York: Catholic Book Publishing Company, 1969), 90.

48. Ibid., 962.

49. Ibid., 1142.

50. Klein, Bence, Campbell, Pearson, and Wimbish, *Growing Up Born Again*, 52-59.

51. Kelly, *Saint Joseph Baltimore Catechism*, 159.

52. Bradley and Kevane, *The Roman Catechism*, 556.

53. Abraham, *Stand Up and fight Back*, 127.

54. Bradley and Kevane, *The Roman Catechism*, 520.

55. Packer, *Concise Theology*, 80-84.

56. New York International Bible Society, *The Holy Bible*, 2-3, 1041-42.

57. National Conference of Catholic Bishops, *The Sacramentary*, 564.

58. Pennock, *This is Our Faith*, 268.

59. Klein, Bence, Campbell, Pearson, and Wimbish, *Growing Up Born Again*, 52.

60. Abraham, *Stand Up and Fight Back*, 118.

61. Packer, *Concise Theology*, 82-84.

62. Pope John Paul II, *Catechism of the Catholic Church*, 563-564, 613-614, 625; Kelly, *Saint Joseph Baltimore Catechism*, 32-33, 109, 130-131; William L. Kelly, *Women Before God*, 3rd ed. (Westminster, MD: The Newman Press, 1961), 183; Abraham, *Stand Up and Fight Back*, 193, 190-196.

63. New York International Bible Society, *The Holy Bible*, 1084-1085.

64. Kelly, *Women Before God*, 183; William L. Kelly, *Men Before God*, 2nd ed. (Westminster, MD: The Newman Press, 1962), 303: Kelly, *Saint Joseph Baltimore Catechism*, 98-99.

65. New York International Bible Society, *The Holy Bible*, 1084, 1096-1097.

66. Abraham, *Stand Up and Fight Back*, 125.

67. Bradley and Kevane, *The Roman Catechism*, 522, 556; Pope John Paul II, *Catechism of the Catholic Church*, 664.

68. Kelly, *Men Before God*, 303; Bradley and Kevane, *The Roman Catechism*, 555.

69. Abraham, *Stand Up and Fight Back*, 99.

70. New York International Bible Society, *The Holy Bible*, 581, 1084-1085; Klein, Bence, Campbell, Pearson, and Wimbish, *Growing Up Born Again*, 77.

71. National Conference of Catholic Bishops, *The Sacramentary*, 270.

72. Stephen Arterburn and Jack Felton, *Faith that Hurts Faith that Heals* (Nashville, TN: Thomas Nelson Publishing, 1991, 1992), 251-252.

73. National Conference of Catholic Bishop, *The Sacramentary*, 269; New York International Bible Society, *The Holy Bible*, 1096.

74. Austin Flannery, gen. ed., *Vatican Council II: The Conciliar and Post Conciliar Documents*, "Lumen Gentium" (Collegeville, MN: Liturgical Press, 1975), 380.

75. Abraham, *Stand Up and Fight Back*, 92.

76. Packer, *Concise Theology*, 16.

77. Vatican Congregation for the Doctrine of the Faith, *Instruction on the Ecclesial Vocation of the Theologian*, May 24, 1990. Full text reprinted in the *National Catholic Reporter*, July 13, 1990 (Vol. 26, #35), paragraph 13.

78. Ibid., paragraph 14.

79. Pennock, *This is Our Faith*, 91.

80. Ibid., 92-93.

81. Ibid., 91.

82. Flannery, *Vatican Council II*, "Lumen Gentium," 383.

83. Ibid., 379.

84. Packer, *Concise Theology*, 17.

85. New York International Bible Society, *The Holy Bible*, 1105.

86. Packer, *Concise Theology*, 17.

87. Klein, Bence, Campbell, Pearson, and Wimbish, *Growing Up Born Again*, 54.

88. Bradley and Kevane, *The Roman Catechism*, 108; Pope John Paul II, *Catechism of the Catholic Church*, 244.

89. Vatican Congregation for the Doctrine of the Faith, *Instruction on the Ecclesial Vocation of the Theologian*, paragraphs 23 and 24; Flannery, *Vatican Council II*, "Lumen Gentium," 379.

90. Flannery, *Vatican Council II*, 379.

91. Pope John Paul II, *Catechism of the Catholic Church*, 562.

92. New York International Bible Society, *The Holy Bible*, 260.

93. Ibid., 1101.

94. Ibid., 1097.

95. Abraham, *Stand Up and Fight Back*, 93.

Chapter 5: Clergy as Healthy Parents

1. Thomas O'Connor and John Gartner, "The Problems and Intimacy in the Priesthood and Religious Life" (Unpublished paper presented to the American Psychological Association, August 11, 1990), 1.

2. James E. Dittes, "Psychological Characteristics of Religious Professionals," in M.P. Strommen, ed., *Research on Religious Development: A Comprehensive Handbook* (New York: Hawthorn, 1971), 423.

3. New York International Bible Society, *The Holy Bible, New International Version* (Grand Rapids, MI: Zondervan Bible Publishers, 1983), 1128.

4. Jack H. Bloom, "Who Became Clergymen?", *Journal of Religion and Health*, (Vol. 10, 1971), 51.

5. C. W. Christensen, "The Occurrence of Mental Illness in the Ministry: Personality Disorders," *Journal of Pastoral Care*, (Vol. 17, 1963), 125-135; L. Morgan, "Mental Illness Among the Clergy: A Survey of State Mental Hospitals in America," *Pastoral Psychology*, (Vol. 9, 1958), 29-36. J. A. M. Kimber, "Interests and Personality Traits of Bible Institute Students," *Journal of Social Psychology*, (Vol. 26, 1947), 225-233.

6. Virginia Celmer and Jane L. Winer, "Female Aspirants to the Roman Catholic Priesthood," *Journal of Counseling and Development*, (Vol. 69, 1990), 178, 181; Philip J. Keddy, Philip Erdberg, and Sean D. Sammon, "The Psychological Assessment of Catholic Clergy and Religious Referred for Residential Treatment," *Pastoral Psychology*, (Vol. 38, No. 3, 1990), 147-159.

7. "Fewer Priests, Sicker Priests, Report," *The Register*, January 13, 1985, 7; William C. Bier, "Basic Rationale for Screening Religious Vocations" in William C. Bier, and A. A. Schneiders, eds., *Selected Papers from the American Catholic Psychological Association Meetings of 1957, 1958, 1959* (New York: Fordham University, 1960), 7-16; T. J. McCarthy, "Personality Traits of Seminarians," *Studies in Psychology and Psychiatry* (Vol. 5, No. 4) (Washington DC: Catholic University of America, 1942).

8. Eugene C. Kennedy and Victor J. Heckler, *The Catholic Priest in the United States: Psychological Investigations* (Washington, DC: United States Catholic Conference, 1972).

9. Ibid., 80.

10. Dittes, "Psychological Characteristics of Religious Professionals," 433, 439.

11. Kennedy and Heckler, *The Catholic Priest in the United States*, 84.

12. Les Steele, "Adult Development Periods and Protestant Male Clergy: A Descriptive Framework," *Journal of Psychology and Theology*, (Vol. 16, No. 1, 1988), 16-17.

13. Ibid.; G. K. Johnson, "Psychological Testing at the Seminary," *Augustana Seminary Review*, (Vol. 4, No. 2, 1952), 18-20; Kennedy and Heckler, *The Catholic Priest in the United States*, 80, 84-85.

14. Bloom, "Who Become Clergymen?", 68-69; K. Sward, "Temperament and Religious Experience," *Journal of Social Psychology*, (Vol. 2, 1931), 374-396.

15. Bloom, "Who Become Clergymen?", 66.

16. Dittes, "Psychological Characteristics of Religious Professionals," 69; O'Connor, and Gartner, "The Problems and Intimacy in the Priesthood and Religious Life," 1-16; Bloom, "Who Become Clergymen?" 64.

17. Dittes, "Psychological Characteristics of Religious Professionals," 445.

18. Bloom, "Who Become Clergymen?", 50-76; Dittes, "Psychological Characteristics of Religious Professionals," 443; C. E. Schroeder, "Personality Patterns of Advanced Protestant Theology Students and Physical Science Students," *Dissertation Abstracts* (Vol. 18, 1958), 154-155; G. E. Whitlock, "The Relationship Between Passivity of Personality and Personal Factors Related to the Choice of Ministry as a Vocation," *Dissertation Abstracts* (Vol. 20, 1959), 2392.

19. Bloom, "Who Become Clergymen?", 71.

20. Philip J. Greven, *The Protestant Temperament* (New York: Alfred A. Knopf, 1977), 32.

21. Philip J. Greven, *Spare the Child* (New York: Alfred Knopf, 1990), 198-199.

22. Greven, *The Protestant Temperament*, 37.

23. F. J. Dodson, "Personality Factors in the Choice of the Protestant Ministry as a Vocation," (Unpublished. PhD Dissertation, University of Southern California, 1957); Howard W. Stone, "Liberals and Conservatives: Differences in Demographic Characteristics, Interests, and Service Orientation Among Those Entering Ministry," *Journal of Psychology and Christianity*, (Vol. 8, No. 3, 1989), 24-37; B. Evans, "A Personality Inventory," (Unpublished D.R.E. Dissertation, New Orleans Baptist Theological Seminary, 1960); Johnson, "Psychological Testing at the Seminary," 18-20; Dittes, "Psychological Characteristics of Religious Professionals," 422-460.

24. Carole A. Rayburn, Lee J. Richmond, and Lynn Rogers, "Men, Women, and Religion: Stress Within Leadership Roles," *Journal of Clinical Psychology*, (Vol. 42, No. 3, 1986), 540-546.

25. Evans, "A Personality Inventory;" G. K. Johnson, "Personality Patterns Peculiar to Theological Students," (Unpublished MA Thesis, University of North Dakota, 1947); Kimber, "Interests and Personality Traits of Bible Institute Students;" G. Stanley, "Personality and Attitude Characteristics of Fundamentalist Theological Students," *Australian Journal of Psychology*, (Vol. 15, 1963), 121-123.

26. Kennedy and Heckler, *The Catholic Priest in the United States*, 106.

27. Rayburn, Richmond, and Rogers, "Men, Women, and Religion: Stress Within Leadership Roles," 544.

28. Bloom, "Who Become Clergymen?", 70, 62.

29. Dittes, "Psychological Characteristics of Religious Professionals," 439; Sward, "Temperament and Religious Experience," 374-396.

30. Allen Nauss, "The Ministerial Personality: Myth or Reality?" *Journal of Religion and Health* (Vol. 12, 1973), 77-96; Dittes, "Psychological Characteristics of Religious Professionals," 449.

31. D. R. Saunders, "Evidence Bearing on the Use of the Myers-Briggs Type Indicator to Select Persons for Advanced Religious Training: A Preliminary Report," *Research Bulletin* (Educational Testing Service), (Vol. 57-58, 1957).

32. Dittes, "Psychological Characteristics of Religious Professionals"; Bloom, "Who Become Clergymen?"

33. McCarthy, "Personality Traits of Seminarians"; Sward, "Temperament and Religious Experience"; P. F. D'Arcy, and Eugene C. Kennedy, *The Genius of the Apostolate* (New York: Sheed and Ward, 1965).

34. Kennedy and Heckler, *The Catholic Priest in the United States*, 85.

35. O'Connor and Gartner, "The Problems and Intimacy in the Priesthood and Religious Life," 8-9; Raymond L. Houck, and Joseph G. Dawson, "Comparative Study of Persisters and Leavers in Seminary Training," *Psychological Reports* (Vol. 42, 1978), 1131-1137.

36. Schroeder, "Personality Patterns of Advanced Protestant Theology Students and Physical Science Students," 154-155.

37. Dodson, "Personality Factors in the Choice of the Protestant Ministry as a Vocation"; O'Connor and Gartner, "The Problems of Intimacy in the Priesthood and Religious Life," 8-9.

38. Greven, *Spare the Child*, 8.

39. Ibid., 49.

40. Ibid., 140-141.

41. Bloom, "Who Become Clergymen?"

42. Ken Abraham, *Stand Up and Fight Back* (Ann Arbor, MI: Servant Publications, 1993), 18.

43. Schroeder, "Personality Patterns of Advanced Protestant Theology Students and Physical Science Students," 154-155; Dodson, "Personality Factors in the Choice of the Protestant Ministry as a Vocation"; Johnson, "Psychological Testing at the Seminary"; O'Connor and Gartner, "The Problems of Intimacy in the Priesthood and Religious Life"; Keddy, Erdberg, and Sammon, "The Psychological Assessment of Catholic Clergy and Religious Referred for Residential Treatment."

44. Greven, *The Protestant Temperament*, 125.

45. Ibid.

46. Ibid.

47. Kennedy and Heckler, *The Catholic Priest in the United States*, 11, 13.

48. Ibid., 81; Evans, "A Personality Inventory."

49. A. W. Richard Sipe, "Newfoundland Report: A Church Reform Manifesto," *National Catholic Reporter*, September 21, 1990, 24.

50. Ibid.

51. Laurence Kohlberg, *Essays on Moral Development: The Psychology of Moral Development* (Vols. I and II) (San Francisco: Harper & Row, 1981, 1984).

52. James W. Fowler, *Stages of Faith* (New York: Harper and Row, 1981).

53. Dennis H. Dirks, "Moral Development in Christian Higher Education," *Journal of Psychology and Theology*, (Vol. 16, No. 4, 1988), 324-331.

54. R. A. Blizard, "The Relationships Between Three Dimensions of Religious Belief and Moral Development," *Dissertation Abstracts International*, (University Microfilms, No. 82-07567) (Vol. 43, 1982), 271B; D. J. Ernsberger, and G. J Manaster, "Moral Development, Intrinsic/Extrinsic Religious Orientation and Denominational Teachings," *Genetic Psychology Monographs* (Vol. 104, 1981), 23-41; R. L. Fleeger, "Critical Thinking and Moral Reasoning Behaviors of Baccalaureate Nursing Students," (Unpublished Doctoral Dissertation, Claremont Graduate School, 1986); D. D. Hoagland, "Moral Judgements and Religious Belief: An Investigation of the Moral Majority," (Unpublished Doctoral Dissertation, Fuller Theological Seminary, 1984).

55. C. McGeorge, "Susceptibility of Faking of the Defining Issues Test," *Developmental Psychology* (Vol. 11, 1975), 108; S. K. Sanderson, "Religion, Politics, and Morality: An Approach to Religious and Political Belief Systems and Their Relation Through Kohlberg's Cognitive Developmental Theory of Moral Judgements," (Unpublished Doctoral Dissertation, University of Nebraska, Lincoln, 1974); I. S Wahrman, "The Relationship of Dogmatism, Religious Affiliation, and Moral Development," *The Journal of Psychology* (Vol. 108, 1981), 151-154; R. J. Wolf, "A Study of the Relationships Between Religious Education, Religious Experience, Maturity, and Moral Development," *Dissertation Abstracts International* (University Microfilms, No. 80-10312) (Vol. 40, 1980), 6219A.

56. New York International Bible Society, *The Holy Bible*, 863.

57. Jeanette A. Lawrence, "Verbal Processing of the Defining Issues Test by Principled and Non-Principled Moral Reasoners," *Journal of Moral Education* (Vol. 16, No. 2, 1987), 129.

58. Kennedy and Heckler, *The Catholic Priest in the United States*, 11.

59. Ibid., 12.

60. Dirks, "Moral Development in Christian Higher Education;" Stanley, "Personality and Attitude Characteristics of Fundamentalist Theological Students."

61. S. W. Blizzard, "The Minister's Dilemma," *Christian Century* (Vol. 73, 1956), 508-509; Celmer and Winer, "Female Aspirants to the Roman Catholic Priesthood," 178-183.

62. Steele, "Adult Development Periods and Protestant Male Clergy: A Descriptive Framework"; H. Newton Malony, "Men and Women in the Clergy: Stresses, Strains, and Resources," *Pastoral Psychology* (Vol. 36, No. 3, 1988).

63. Ibid., 165.

64. Ibid., 167.

65. Bishops' Committee on Priestly Life and Ministry, *Reflections on the Morale of Priests* (Washington, DC: United States Catholic Conference, 1985), 17.

66. Ibid., 5.

67. Claudia J. Postell, "Clergy Malpractice: An Emerging Field of Law," *Trial* (December, 1985), 91, 93; Malony, "Men and

Women in the Clergy: Stresses, Strains, and Resources," 167; Edward Barker, and Allen P. Wilkinson, "Clergy Malpractice: Cloaked by the Cloth?" Trial (May 1990), 36-40.

68. Tom Morton, "Convictions in Investment Scheme," Christianity Today (Vol. 37, No. 11, 1993), 57.

69. "Clerical Malpractice: Faith or Fraud," The Economist (Vol. 295, 1985), 28-29; Elinor Burkett, and Frank Bruni, A Gospel of Shame: Children, Sexual Abuse and the Catholic Church (New York: Viking, 1993), 205-206.

70. Burkett and Bruni, A Gospel of Shame, 38, 40, 257.

71. Randy Frame, "Time to Tighten Purse Strings," Christianity Today (Vol. 37, No. 1, October 4, 1993); Andrew Greeley, "Where Have All the Contributions Gone? And Why?", National Catholic Reporter (Nov. 11, 1988), 17.

72. Burkett and Bruni, A Gospel of Shame, 206; Harvey Cox, "If You Think Rome is Going Conservative, Look At Us Baptists," National Catholic Reporter (September 4, 1987), 12-13.

73. Richard A. Schoenherr and Andrew M. Greeley, "Role Commitment Processes and the American Priesthood," American Sociological Review, (Vol. 39, 1974), 407-426.

74. Thomas J. Murphy, "The Relationship Between Self-Actualization and Adjustment Among American Catholic Priests," Educational and Psychological Measurement, (Vol. 40, 1980), 457-461.

75. Kennedy and Heckler, The Catholic Priest in the United States, 105.

PART TWO: ONE BIG HAPPY FAMILY

Introduction

1. Joseph H. Brown and Dana N. Christensen, Family Therapy: Theory and Practice (Monterey, CA: Brooks/Cole, 1986), 11.

2. Dorothy Stroh Becvar and Raphael J. Becvar, Family Therapy: A Systemic Integration (Boston, MA: Allyn and Bacon, 1988), 11.

Chapter 6: What Will People Think?

1. Barbara F. Okun and Louis J. Rappaport, Working with Families: An Introduction to Family Therapy (North Scituate, MA: Duxbury Press, 1980), 114.

2. Irene Goldenberg and Herbert Goldenberg, *Family Therapy: An Overview*, 3rd ed. (Monterey, CA: Brooks/Cole, 1991), 149.

3. Alexandra G. Kaplan, "The 'Self-in-Relation': Implications for Depression in Women," in Judith V. Jordan, Alexandra G. Kaplan, Jean Baker Miller, Irene P. Stiver, and Janet L. Surrey, eds., *Women's Growth in Connection* (New York: The Guilford Press, 1991), 206.

4. Goldenberg and Goldenberg, *Family Therapy*, 148-149; Joseph H. Brown, and Dana N. Christensen, *Family Therapy: Theory and Practice* (Monterey, CA: Brooks/Cole, 1986), 121-122.

5. Ronald L. Levant, *Family Therapy: A Comprehensive Overview* (Englewood Cliffs, NJ: Prentice-Hall, 1984), 103.

6. Dorothy Stroh Becvar, and Raphael J. Becvar, *Family Therapy: A Systemic Integration* (Boston, MA: Allyn and Bacon, 1988), 136.

7. Okun and Rappaport, *Working with Families*, 115.

Chapter 7: To Thine Own Self Be Untrue

1. Joseph H. Brown and Dana N. Christensen, *Family Therapy: Theory and Practice* (Monterey, CA: Brooks/Cole, 1986), 120.

2. Ibid., 120-121.

3. Ronald L. Levant, *Family Therapy: A Comprehensive Overview* (Englewood Cliffs, NJ: Prentice-Hall, 1984), 110-111.

4. Ibid., 112-113.

5. Ibid., 113.

6. Irene Goldenberg and Herbert Goldenberg, *Family Therapy: An Overview*, 3rd ed. (Monterey, CA: Brooks/Cole, 1991), 36.

7. Barbara F. Okun and Louis J. Rappaport, *Working with Families: An Introduction to Family Therapy* (North Scituate, MA: Duxbury Press, 1980), 90-91.

8. Ibid.

9. Levant, *Family Therapy*, 111.

10. Susan Forward, *Toxic Parents: Overcoming Their Hurtful Legacy and Reclaiming Your Life* (New York: Bantam Books, 1989), 174.

Chapter 8: Spinning a Web

1. Irene Goldenberg, and Herbert Goldenberg, *Family Therapy: An Overview*, 3rd ed. (Monterey, CA: Brooks/Cole, 1991), 151.

2. Barbara F. Okun and Louis J. Rappaport, *Working with Families: An Introduction to Family Therapy* (North Scituate, MA: Duxbury Press, 1980), 117; Ronald L. Levant, *Family Therapy: A Comprehensive Overview* (Englewood Cliffs, NJ: Prentice-Hall, 1984), 104.

3. Dorothy Stroh Becvar and Raphael J. Becvar, *Family Therapy: A Systemic Integration* (Boston, MA: Allyn and Bacon, 1988), 137.

Chapter 9: Scapegoating

1. Joseph H. Brown and Dana N. Christensen, *Family Therapy: Theory and Practice* (Monterey, CA: Brooks/Cole, 1986), 63, 300.

2. Ibid.; Ronald L. Levant, *Family Therapy: A Comprehensive Overview* (Englewood Cliffs, NJ: Prentice-Hall, 1984), 62-63.

3. Levant, *Family Therapy*, 91.

4. Ibid.

5. Irene Goldenberg and Herbert Goldenberg, *Family Therapy: An Overview*, 3rd ed. (Monterey, CA: Brooks/Cole, 1991), 173; Levant, 62.

6. Goldenberg and Goldenberg, *Family Therapy*, 102.

7. Barbara Cottman Becnel, *The Co-Dependent Parent: Free Yourself by Freeing Your Child* (San Francisco: Harper, 1991), 78.

8. Luciano L'Abate, Gary Ganahl, and James C. Hansen, *Methods of Family Therapy* (Englewood Cliffs, NJ: Prentice-Hall, 1986), 17.

Chapter 10: Shadow Carriers

1. Irene Goldenberg and Herbert Goldenberg, *Family Therapy: An Overview*, 3rd ed. (Monterey, CA: Brooks/Cole, 1991), 154.

2. Robert H. Hopcke, *Jung, Jungians and Homosexuality* (Boston: Shambhala, 1989), 110, 118-119, 171.

3. Ibid.

4. Eugene C. Kennedy and Victor J. Heckler, *The Catholic Priest in the United States: Psychological Investigations* (Washington, DC: United States Catholic Conference, 1972), 7-13.

5. Eugene Kennedy, "Asexuality Seen in Power Moves on U.S. Church," *National Catholic Reporter* (November 4, 1986).

6. John Boswell, *Christianity, Social Tolerance and Homosexuality* (Chicago: The University of Chicago Press, 1980), 187-193; 210-228.

7. James G. Wolf, ed., *Gay Priests* (New York: Harper & Row, 1989), 59-76.

8. A. W. Richard Sipe, *A Secret World: Sexuality and the Search for Celibacy* (New York: Brunner/Mazel, 1990), 107, 117.

9. Richard P. McBrien, "Homosexuality and the Priesthood: Questions We Can't Keep in the Closet," *Commonweal* (June 19, 1987), 380-383.

10. Ronald L. Levant, *Family Therapy: A Comprehensive Overview* (Englewood Cliffs, NJ: Prentice-Hall, 1984), 95; Irene Goldenberg and Herbert Goldenberg, *Family Therapy: An Overview*, 3rd ed. (Monterey, CA: Brooks/Cole, 1991), 101-102; James W. Jones, *Contemporary Psychoanalysis and Religion: Transference and Transcendence* (New Haven, CT: Yale University Press, 1991), 29.

Chapter 11: A Disowned Past

1. Dorothy Stroh Becvar and Raphael J. Becvar, *Family Therapy: A Systemic Integration* (Boston, MA: Allyn and Bacon, 1988), 138. Irene Goldenberg and Herbert Goldenberg, *Family Therapy: An Overview*, 3rd ed. (Monterey, CA: Brooks/Cole, 1991), 155.

2. Murray Bowen, *Family Therapy in Clinical Practice* (New York: Jason Aronson, 1978); Joseph H. Brown, and Dana L. Christensen, *Family Therapy: Theory and Practice* (Monterey, CA: Brooks/Cole, 1986), 24-25.

3. Becvar and Becvar, *Family Therapy*, 138.

4. Barbara F. Okun and Louis J. Rappaport, *Working with Families: An Introduction to Family Therapy* (North Scituate, MA: Duxbury Press, 1980), 119.

5. James Framo, "The Integration of Marital Therapy with Sessions with Family of Origin," in A. Gurman and D. Kniskern, eds., *Handbook of Family Therapy* (New York: Brunner/Mazel, 1981); Brown and Christensen, *Family Therapy*, 118.

6. Ronald L. Levant, *Family Therapy: A Comprehensive Overview* (Englewood Cliffs, NJ: Prentice-Hall, 1984), 105.

7. Goldenberg and Goldenberg, *Family Therapy*, 148-150.

8. Levant, *Family Therapy*, 105.

9. Goldenberg and Goldenberg, *Family Therapy*, 155.

Chapter 12: Don't Rock the Boat

1. Irene Goldenberg and Herbert Goldenberg, *Family Therapy: An Overview*, 3rd ed. (Monterey, CA: Brooks/Cole, 1991), 38.
2. Ibid., 43.

Chapter 13: Caught in the Middle

1. Barbara F. Okun and Louis J. Rappaport, *Working with Families: An Introduction to Family Therapy* (North Scituate, MA: Duxbury Press, 1980), 142.
2. Luciano L'Abate, Gary Ganahl, and James C. Hansen, *Methods of Family Therapy* (Englewood Cliffs, NJ:, Prentice-Hall, 1986), 21.
3. Joseph H. Brown and Dana N. Christensen, *Family Therapy: Theory and Practice* (Monterey, CA: Brooks/Cole, 1986), 144.
4. Irene Goldenberg and Herbert Goldenberg, *Family Therapy: An Overview*, 3rd ed. (Monterey, CA: Brooks/Cole, 1991), 170.
5. Virginia Satir, *Conjoint Family Therapy* (Palo Alto, CA: Science and Behavior Books, 1967), 185.
6. Jim Castelli, "Bishops Begin to Tackle the Stress that Faces Them," *National Catholic Reporter*, August 24, 1990, 5-6.

Chapter 14: Business as Usual

1. Irene Goldenberg and Herbert Goldenberg, *Family Therapy: An Overview*, 3rd ed. (Monterey, CA: Brooks/Cole, 1991), 41.
2. Luciano L'Abate, Gary Ganahl, and James C. Hansen, *Methods of Family Therapy* (Englewood Cliffs, NJ: Prentice-Hall, 1986), 12.
3. Joseph H. Brown and Dana N. Christensen, *Family Therapy: Theory and Practices* (Monterey, CA: Brooks/Cole, 1986), 12.
4. Goldenberg and Goldenberg, *Family Therapy*, 46.
5. Ibid., 43.
6. Ronald L. Levant, *Family Therapy: A Comprehensive Overview* (Englewood Cliffs, NJ: Prentice-Hall, 1984), 14.

Chapter 15: Speaking with Forked Tongue

1. Irene Goldenberg and Herbert Goldenberg, *Family Therapy: An Overview*, 3rd ed. (Monterey, CA: Brooks/Cole, 1991), 185-186.

2. Dorothy Stroh Becvar and Raphael J. Becvar, *Family Therapy: A Systemic Integration* (Boston, MA: Allyn and Bacon, 1988), 21-22; Ronald F. Levant, *Family Therapy: A Comprehensive Overview* (Englewood Cliffs, NJ: Prentice-Hall, 1984), 55-56; Barbara F. Okun and Louis J. Rappaport, *Working with Families: An Introduction to Family Therapy* (North Scituate, MA: Duxbury Press, 1980), 42.

Chapter 16: Challenges to the Power Structure

1. Irene Goldenberg and Herbert Goldenberg, *Family Therapy: An Overview*, 3rd ed. (Monterey, CA: Brooks/Cole, 1991), 328.
2. Ibid., 171.
3. Ibid., 44.
4. Joseph H. Brown and Dana N. Christensen, *Family Therapy: Theory and Practice* (Monterey, CA: Brooks/Cole, 1986), 62, 84-89.
5. Dorothy Stroh Becvar and Raphael J. Becvar, *Family Therapy: A Systemic Integration* (Boston, MA: Allyn and Bacon, 1988), 223.
6. Luciano L'Abate, Gary Ganahl, and James C. Hansen, *Methods of Family Therapy* (Englewood Cliffs, NJ: Prentice-Hall, 1986), 17.

PART THREE: CLAIMING YOUR OWN VOICE

Chapter 17: Grieving Illusions

1. John McDargh, *Psychoanalytic Object Relations Theory and the Study of Religion* (Lanham, MD: University Press of America, 1983), 79; Randall Lehmann Sorenson, "The Process of Change in Psychoanalytic Theory: Implication for Analysis of Religious Experience" (Unpublished paper, presented at a Division 36 Symposium, American Psychological Association, August 16, 1992), 7.
2. James F. Masterson, *The Real Self* (New York: Brunner/ Mazel, 1985), 40; James F. Masterson, *The Search for the Real Self* (New York: The Free Press, 1988), 61.
3. Craig O'Neill and Kathleen Ritter, *Coming Out Within: Stages of Spiritual Awakening for Lesbians and Gay Men* (San Francisco: Harper, 1992), 54.

4. The eight-stage loss model discussed in this book is adapted from John Schneider, *Stress, Loss, and Grief* (Baltimore: University Park Press, 1984); and John Schneider, *Finding My Way: Healing and Transformation through Loss and Grief* (Colfax, WI: Seasons Press, 1994); O'Neill and Ritter used the model as the framework for *Coming Out Within.*

5. O'Neill and Ritter, *Coming Out Within*, 95.

6. Schneider, *Stress, Loss, and Grief*, 162.

7. Ibid., 181.

8. Ibid., 183.

9. Ibid., 190.

10. New York International Bible Society, *The Holy Bible, New International Version* (Grand Rapids, MI: Zondervan Bible Publishers, 1983), 1102.

11. Ibid., 911.

12. Masterson, *The Search for the Real Self*, 42-46.

13. Schneider, *Stress, Loss, and Grief*, 184.

14. James W. Jones, *Contemporary Psychoanalysis and Religion: Transference and Transcendence* (New Haven, CT: Yale University Press, 1991), 103.

15. Anita L. Sorenson, "Psychoanalytic Perspectives on Religion: The Illusion Has a Future," *Journal of Psychology and Theology.* (Vol. 18), 216.

Chapter 18: Living with Paradox

1. Pytyia Peay, "Campbell and Catholicism," *Common Boundary,* (Vol. 10, 1992), 32-33.

2. Ibid., 33.

3. Richard McBrien, "Issues Consuming Church Not Gospel Imperatives," *National Catholic Reporter,* (Vol. 30, #37, 1994), 2.

4. John Schneider, *Stress, Loss, and Grief* (Baltimore, MD: University Park Press, 1984), 193-206; John Schneider, *Finding My Way: Healing and Transformation Through Loss and Grief* (Colfax WI: Seasons Press, 1994), 199-229.

5. Schneider, *Stress, Loss, and Grief*, 194.

6. Schneider, *Finding My Way*, 200.

7. Schneider, *Stress, Loss, and Grief*, 207-227; Schneider, *Finding My Way*, 231-261.

8. John McDargh, *Psychoanalytic Object Relations Theory and the Study of Religion* (Lanham, MD: University Press of America, 1983), 95.

9. Dana Crowley Jack, *Silencing the Self: Women and Depression* (Cambridge, MA: Harvard University Press, 1991), 195-197.

10. Ibid., 195.

11. Ibid., 205.

12. John McDargh, *Psychoanalytic Object Relations Theory and the Study of Religion*, 89.

Chapter 19: Transforming Illusions

1. James W. Fowler, *Stages of Faith: The Psychology of Human Development and the Quest for Meaning* (San Francisco: Harper and Row, 1981), 197-198.

2. Ibid.

3. James W. Jones, *Contemporary Psychoanalysis and Religion: Transference and Transcendence* (New Haven, CT: Yale University Press, 1991); Ana Maria Rizzuto, *The Birth of the Living God: A Psychoanalytic Study* (Chicago: The University of Chicago Press, 1979).

4. Jones, *Contemporary Psychoanalysis and Religion*, 81.

5. James W. Fowler, *Stages of Faith: The Psychology of Human Development and the Quest for Meaning*, 121; Jones, *Contemporary Psychoanalysis and Religion*, 82; John McDargh, *Psychoanalytic Object Relations Theory and the Study of Religion*, (Lanham, MD: University Press of America, 1983), 141-148; Rizzuto, *The Birth of the Living God*, 178, 185-188.

6. Rizzuto, *The Birth of the Living God*, 45.

7. McDargh, *Psychoanalytic Object Relations Theory and the Study of Religion*, 120.

8. Ibid.

9. Ibid., 219-220.

10. Fowler, *Stages of Faith*, 121.

11. Erik M. Erikson, "The Development of Ritualization," in Donald R. Cutler, ed., *The Religious Situation 1968* (Boston: Beacon Press, 1968).

12. D. W. Winnicott, "The Theory of the Parent-Infant Relationship," *International Journal of Psychoanalysis*, Vol. 41, 1960),

585-595; Christopher Bollas, *The Shadow of the Object: Psycho-analysis of the Unthought Known* (New York: Columbia University Press, 1987), 14-18.

13. New York International Bible Society, *The Holy Bible, New International Version* (Grand Rapids, MI: Zondervan Bible Publishers, 1983), 1068, 572, 681, 697, 501.

14. The International Commission on English in the Liturgy, *The Rites of the Catholic Church* (New York: Pueblo, 1983), 302.

15. Ibid., 203.

16. National Conference of Catholic Bishops, *The Sacramentary* (The Roman Missal Revised) (New York: Catholic Book Publishing Company, 1974), 501.

17. McDargh, *Psychoanalytic Object Relations Theory and the Study of Religion*, 219.

18. Erik M. Erikson, *Insight and Responsibility: Lectures on the Ethical Implications of Psychoanalytic Insight* (New York: W. W. Norton, 1964), 118.

19. McDargh, *Psychoanalytic Object Relations Theory and the Study of Religion*, 224.

20. James Masterson, *The Real Self* (New York: Brunner/Mazel, 1985), 29.

21. Fowler, *Stages of Faith*, 121.

22. Rizzuto, *The Birth of the Living God*, 185-188.

23. Jones, *Contemporary Psychoanalysis and Religion*, 64-65, 88.

24. Heinz Kohut, *The Restoration of the Self* (New York: International Universities Press, 1977), 49.

25. Fowler, *Stages of Faith*, 121.

26. Jones, *Contemporary Psychoanalysis and Religion*, 43.

27. Rizzuto, *The Birth of the Living God*, 121.

28. New York International Bible Society, *The Holy Bible*, 2.

29. National Conference of Catholic Bishops, *The Sacramentary*, 346.

30. New York International Bible Society, *The Holy Bible*, 127.

31. Ibid., 516, 507, 547.

32. Ibid., 1064.

33. Ibid., 1069.

34. Ibid., 513, 561.

35. Ibid, 505, 911.

36. Ibid., 504, 505, 513, 515, 525, 551, 560, 582.

37. Fowler, *Stages of Faith*, 53-55, 120-121.

38. Jones, *Contemporary Psychoanalysis and Religion*, 17, 116; Bollas, *The Shadow of the Object*, 3.

39. McDargh, *Psychoanalytic Object Relations Theory and the Study of Religion*, 225, 225-230.

40. Ibid., 226.

41. Bollas, *The Shadow of the Object*, 14; Jones, *Contemporary Psychoanalysis and Religion*, 116.

42. Jones, *Contemporary Psychoanalysis and Religion*, 105, 59; McDargh, *Psychoanalytic Object Relations Theory and the Study of Religion*, 213.

43. Ana Maria Rizzuto, "Conclusion from Birth of the Living God," in Margaret Gorman, ed., *Psychology and Religion* (Mahwah, NJ: Paulist Press, 1985), 125; McDargh, *Psychoanalytic Object Relations Theory and the Study of Religion*, 227-230.

44. Rizzuto, *The Birth of the Living God*, 45.

45. McDargh, *Psychoanalytic Object Relations Theory and the Study of Religion*, 123.

46. Ibid., 229.

47. Ibid., 230; Fowler, *Stages of Faith*, 121.

48. McDargh, *Psychoanalytic Object Relations Theory and the Study of Religion*, 230-235.

49. Jones, *Contemporary Psychoanalysis and Religion*, 121; Bollas, *The Shadow of the Object*, 14-17.

50. Jones, *Contemporary Psychoanalysis and Religion*, 83.

51. Ibid., 82-83; Bollas, *The Shadow of the Object*, 14-17.

52. Jones, *Contemporary Psychoanalysis and Religion*, 104-108.

53. New York International Bible Society, *The Holy Bible*, 511-512, 994, 1048.

54. Ibid., 673.

55. Ibid., 553, 575.

56. Ibid., 865.

57. Pope John Paul II, *Catechism of the Catholic Church* (New York: Image Doubleday, 1995), 6, 63-66, 64, 111.

58. National Conference of Catholic Bishops, *The Sacramentary*, 21, 564, 547.

59. Ibid., 563.

60. W. W. Meissner, *Psychoanalysis and Religious Experience*, (New Haven, CT: Yale University Press, 1984) 182.

61. Ana Maria Rizzuto, *The Birth of the Living God*; Jones, *Contemporary Psychoanalysis and Religion*.

62. Bollas, *The Shadow of the Object*, 14.

63. McDargh, *Psychoanalytic Object Relations Theory and the Study of Religion*, 81-84.

64. Ibid., 230.

65. John M. Maher and Dennie Briggs, eds., *An Open Life: Joseph Campbell in Conversation with Michael Toms* (Burdett, NY: Larson Publications, 1988).

66. W. W. Meissner, *Psychoanalysis and Religious Experience*, 181.

67. Bollas, *The Shadow of the Object*, 16.

68. Ibid., 17.

69. Moshe Halevi Spero, *Religious Objects as Psychological Structures* (Chicago: The University of Chicago Press, 1992).

70. Joseph Campbell, *Myths to Live By*, (New York: Viking, 1972).

71. Maher and Briggs, *An Open Life*, 117.

72. Ibid., 68-69.

73. Miriam Therese Winter, *Woman Prayer Woman Song* (Oak Park, IL: Meyer Stone, 1987), 9.

74. Ibid., 5, 9.

75. Meissner, *Psychoanalysis and Religious Experience*, 182.

76. Spero, *Religious Objects as Psychological Structures*, 65, 66, 74.

77. Campbell, *Myths to Live By*, 104.

78. Fowler, *Stages of Faith: The Psychology of Human Development and the Quest for Meaning*, 198.

79. Winter, *Woman Prayer Woman Song*, 10-11.

80. Rosemary Radford Ruether, *Women-Church: Theology and Practice of Feminist Liturgical Communities* (San Francisco: Harper & Row, 1985).

Index

MORE BOOKS ON *RELIGION, MINISTRY & PASTORAL CARE*

TAKE 20% OFF ON EACH BOOK!

Special Sale!

RIGHTEOUS RELIGION
Unmasking the Illusions of Fundamentalism and Authoritarian Catholicism
Kathleen Ritter and Craig O'Neill
$17.95 hard. ISBN: 0-7890-6016-7.
(Outside US/Canada/Mexico: $22.00)
Available Summer 1996. Approx. 173 pp.

THEOLOGICAL CONTEXT FOR PASTORAL CAREGIVING
Word in Deed
The Rev. Howard W. Stone, PhD
$29.95 hard. ISBN: 0-7890-0072-5.
(Outside US/Canada/Mexico: $36.00)
$19.95 soft. ISBN: 0-7890-0125-X
(Outside US/Canada/Mexico: $24.00)
Available Summer 1996. Approx. 160 pp. with Index.

ECOTHERAPY
Healing Ourselves, Healing the Earth
Howard Clinebell, PhD
" *Critically significant book to be read by therapists, educators and people of all faiths who seek to be instruments of healing today and into the twenty-first century. Truly a 'must' for all who care about living together on this Mother-Father Earth.*"
—*EarthLight Magazine*
Co-published with Fortress Press.
$17.95 soft. ISBN: 0-7890-6009-4.
(Outside US/Canada/Mexico: $22.00)
Available Spring 1996. Approx. 350 pp. with Index.

COUNSELING FOR SPIRITUALLY EMPOWERED WHOLENESS
A Hope-Centered Approach
Howard Clinebell, PhD
An introduction to Wholeness Counseling (also called Growth Counseling), a whole-person approach to pastoral counseling.
$29.95 hard. ISBN: 1-56024-902-1.
(Outside US/Canada/Mexico: $36.00)
$14.95 soft. ISBN: 1-56024-903-X.
(Outside US/Canada/Mexico: $18.00)
1995. 177 pp. with Index.
A previous edition of this book was published under the title *Growth Counseling*.

DEALING WITH DEPRESSION
Five Pastoral Interventions
Richard Dayringer, ThD
This important book explores strategies to enable clergy to identify and help individuals suffering from depression to cope more successfully.
$29.95 hard. ISBN: 1-56024-933-1.
(Outside US/Canada/Mexico: $36.00)
$12.95 soft. ISBN: 1-56024-967-6.
(Outside US/Canada/Mexico: $16.00)
1995. 175 pp. with Index.

SHAME
A Faith Perspective
Robert H. Albers, PhD
In this important guidebook, author Robert H. Albers provides both an analysis of and a Biblical and theological reflection upon the human experience of disgrace shame.
$29.95 hard. ISBN: 1-56024-935-8.
(Outside US/Canada/Mexico: $36.00)
$12.95 soft. ISBN: 1-56024-957-9.
(Outside US/Canada/Mexico: $16.00)
1995. 148 pp. with Index

AGING AND GOD
Spiritual Pathways to Mental Health in Midlife and Later Years
Harold G. Koenig, MD, MHSc
"*The text is user-friendly. . . . Statistics are graphed or charted but also explained well in the text so the lay reader need not feel overwhelmed.*"
—*Church & Synagogue Libraries*
$79.95 hard. ISBN: 1-56024-423-2.
(Outside US/Canada/Mexico: $96.00)
$19.95 soft. ISBN: 1-56024-424-0.
(Outside US/Canada/Mexico: $24.00)
1994. 544 pp. with Indexes.

Faculty: Textbooks are available for classroom adoption consideration on a 60–day examination basis. You will receive an invoice payable within 60 days along with the book. **If you decide to adopt the book, your invoice will be cancelled.** Please write to us on your institutional letterhead, indicating the textbook you would like to examine as well as the following information: course title, current text, enrollment, and decision date. *(See order form on reverse side)*

The Haworth Pastoral Press
An imprint of the The Haworth Press, Inc.
10 Alice Street, Binghamton, New York 13904–1580 USA

HORRIFIC TRAUMATA

A Pastoral Response to the
Post-Traumatic Stress Disorder
N. Duncan Sinclair, MDiv
"Outlines how pastoral counselors and others can help
heal the isolation and trauma and promote growth. "
–Library Journal
$39.95 hard. ISBN: 1-56024-293-0.
(Outside US/Canada/Mexico: $48.00)
$12.95 soft. ISBN: 1-56024-294-9.
(Outside US/Canada/Mexico: $16.00)
1993. 120 pp. with Index.

VICTIMS OF DEMENTIA

Services, Support, and Care
William Michael Clemmer, PhD
"Common sense approach, easy reading, specific day-to-
day details of operation, and extensive appendixes. "
—Clinical Gerontologist
$29.95 hard. ISBN: 1-56024-264-7.
(Outside US/Canada/Mexico: $36.00)
$19.95 soft. ISBN: 1-56024-265-5.
(Outside US/Canada/Mexico: $24.00)
1993. 155 pp. with Index.

RELIGION AND THE FAMILY

When God Helps
Edited by Laurel Arthur Burton, ThD
"Affords practical approaches to making faith an
important part of therapy."
—The American Journal of Family Therapy
$29.95 hard. ISBN: 1-56024-192-6.
(Outside US/Canada/Mexico: $36.00)
$19.95 soft. ISBN: 1-56024-197-7.
(Outside US/Canada/Mexico: $24.00)
1992. 215 pp. with Index.

GROWING UP

Pastoral Nurture for the Later Years
Thomas B. Robb, ThD
"Gives the reader some searching insight into the personal
and spiritual dimensions of growing up and growing old.
Recommended for chaplains and pastors."
—NAVAC
$39.95 hard. ISBN: 1-56024-072-5.
(Outside US/Canada/Mexico: $48.00)
$12.95 soft. ISBN: 1-56024-073-3.
(Outside US/Canada/Mexico: $16.00)
1991. 148 pp. with Index.

TAKE 20% OFF ON EACH BOOK!

Special Sale!

CALL OUR TOLL-FREE NUMBER: 1–800–342–9678
US & Canada only / 9am–5pm ET; Monday–Friday
FAX YOUR ORDER TO US: 1–800–895–0582
Outside US/Canada: + 607–722–6362
E-MAIL YOUR ORDER TO US: getinfo@haworth.com

Order Today and Save!

The Haworth Press, Inc.
10 Alice Street, Binghamton New York 13904–1580 USA